A LIFE OF A PHYSICIST IN AGRICULTURAL RESEARCH

A Professional Autobiography

'Upholding spirituality and complementarity by society through all ages'

Concept design by Anil Vishnu Moharir

A LIFE OF A PHYSICIST IN AGRICULTURAL RESEARCH

A Professional Autobiography

ANIL VISHNU MOHARIR

Published by Zorba Books, July 2022
Website: www.zorbabooks.com
Email: info@zorbabooks.com

Title:- **A LIFE OF A PHYSICIST IN AGRICULTURAL RESEARCH**

Printbook ISBN :- 978-93-93029-20-1
Ebook ISBN :- 978-93-93029-30-0

Zorba Books Pvt. Ltd. (opc)
Sushant Arcade,
Next to Courtyard Marriot,
Sushant Lok 1, Gurgaon – 122009, India

Printed by Thomson Press (India) Ltd.
B-315, Okhla Industrial Area, Phase 1, New Delhi- 110020

Dedicated to my wife Sulochana Moharir who has stood by me all through my years of struggle, tribulations, moments of joy, achievements and now in blissful solitude.

Anil Vishnu Moharir

March 13, 2013
New Delhi

Table of Contents

Foreword to the Second Edition

Dayalbagh Educational Institute
(Deemed-to-be University)
Online & Distance Education Centre

Prof. V. B. Gupta,
Coordinator

Foreword

A remarkable feature of this book entitled 'A Life of a Physicist in Agricultural Research' by Prof. Anil Vishnu Moharir is that once you start reading it, you don't like to put it aside. The author has created a fabric of exquisite beauty through interweaving of physics and agriculture as warp and weft. The resulting procedures, techniques, processes and products are described in the book. It is interesting to note that like a good story – teller, the author uses simple language to tell about complex scientific events ensuring that the story continues to arouse curiosity in the reader and keep his interest alive.

I have had the privilege of knowing Dr. A. V. Moharir for over 45 years now –first as a Ph.D. student and then as a colleague. Dr. Moharir was first introduced to me in the year 1975 when he was working as an Assistant Physicist (Electron microscope) in the Prestigious Indian Agricultural Research Institute (IARI), New Delhi. I was then a faculty member in the Textile Department of IIT, Delhi and keen to have a student studying for Ph.D. on a natural fibre – preferably cotton. Mr. Anil Vishnu Moharir fitted the bill very well. The story of his Ph.D. journey has been ably covered by him in the book. I found him to be an intelligent, hardworking student who displayed unusual commitment and kept targets. As a result, we were able to have several excellent publications in reputed journals from the research work done.

I made several visits to the Electron Microscope Laboratory of Dr. Moharir in IARI and we had very detailed scientific discussions during these visits.

They had developed several techniques for sample preparation for transmission electron microscopy study and also the contact electron micrography for characterization of thin films and paper.

There are several other areas in which Dr. Moharir and his group have done commendable work. These include (i) development of significant and very accurate spectro-photometric methods for determination of trace elements, viz. iron and titanium in soils, plants, etc.

i. Identification of crystallite orientation through X-ray diffraction in cotton varieties as a benchmark for fibre strength, and
ii. Use of moisture absorption / desorption curves (hysteresis curves) to characterize drought – resistance of wheat crops.

Besides the above, there are several other noteworthy developments reported by Dr. Moharir in the book: Anyone going through this book will have admiration for the author for his multi-faceted contributions in the field of Agriculture through physics and physical methods and will come out with the conviction that multidisciplinary approach can lead to innovative observations and discoveries which cannot be possible if one sticks to a single discipline.

Dr. Moharir has been very active after retirement by contributing through publishing articles on a variety of subjects, mainly dealing with scientific and religions aspects.

I feel privileged to have been asked to write this Foreword. I would like to make it clear that my comments are limited to the role played by a physicist in agricultural research and should not be taken to mean that I subscribe to his views expressed on the political and social issues in this book.

VB Gupta

Dayalbagh, Agra – 282005 **(V.B. Gupta)**

June 28, 2022

Foreword to the First Edition

National Academy of Agricultural Sciences

FOREWORD

Prof. R.B. Singh
President

This book, 'A Life of a Physicist in Agricultural Research' by Professor Anil Vishnu Moharir, is a rich chronicle of the pioneering research work done by a physicist in the field of agriculture, an area of which he had no formal education and training. It is interesting to read, how the author not only got his foothold but contributed in a significant way. The infrastructure, facilities, environment and opportunities provided by the world famous Indian Agricultural Research Institute (IARI), New Delhi, had also contributed to the success of the author, which he magnanimously acknowledges. Personally, I am privileged to have walked with Prof. Moharir for several years in his journey at IARI.

The author has put the whole narration in a very succinct and precise perspective and one would find it quite hard to cut portions in selective reading. As perceived from the appended list of his research papers, books and articles, he has been very modest in stating his research achievements in the multidisciplinary approach to agricultural research for development. Reading through the description on sundry experiments, several techniques or procedures developed by him, such as the concept of normalized moisture hysteresis and structure-property relations in cotton fibres of different varieties and species are verily enriching. As a cotton breeder myself in the early part of my scientific research career, I personally felt the need for more extensive research in exploiting the use of the Herman's crystallite orientation factor identified by Dr. Moharir as an index for screening cotton germplam and breeding new varieties with high inherent tensile strength of fibres. As the cotton economy and industry is revolutionising fast, the lead provided by the author should be judiciously harnessed.

NASC
DPS Marg, P.O. Pusa
New Delhi 110 012

Tel: 91-11-25846055
91-11-25846051
91-11-25846052
Fax 91-11-25846054
Email: naas@vsnl.com
Web.: www.naasindia.org

The book amply reveals the emotion, enthusiasm, joy and commitment of a research scientist in exploring newer ideas. Occasional references to other fields of science, science policy issues, philosophy, religion and history are not only inevitable and relevant, but also underpin that science does not work in a vacuum and has a human, cultural, economic and environmental face. Effective execution and implementation of outcome of such humanised sciences go a long way in encouraging or creating a congenial atmosphere of cooperation for progress in general and creative scientific research in particular. The book beautifully describes the importance of a holistic and multi-disciplinary (agriculture, physics, engineering and humanities) approach to scientific problems in a very lucid language.

The author, as a young boy of three plus holding the tricolour in his hand welcomed India's Independence in 1947, and has all along keenly witnessed the national development. Having chosen to serve the society through science, some of the points made by him may not be acceptable to all, but, in retrospect one would always find these as reflections of a young budding scientist who had been inflamed with imagination, inspiration and aspiration for speedy development of an impoverished country.

The centrality of the role of basic sciences, especially the congruence of physical, chemical and biological sciences in paving the way for science-led growth and development can hardly be overemphasised. It is this congruence which led to the discovery of DNA double helix and the central dogma, molecular biology, biotechnology, bioinformatics, and nanotechnology which are transforming the world. This fact needs to be duly appreciated in the field of agricultural research and education and necessary arrangement should be made to strengthen teaching of basic sciences as well as recruitment of needed experts in agricultural universities and institutions.

The National Academy of Agricultural Sciences (NAAS) in its recent policy papers and conferences has vigorously flagged the issue of strengthening basic sciences in agricultural universities and suggested the way forward. In this context, I admire the effort put in by Professor Moharir which must motivate many young and bright students of physics and other basic sciences to foray in the field of biology and agriculture for a satisfying career and opportunities for innovative original research to their credit. At the same time, it must motivate agricultural scientists to adopt a multi-disciplinary outlook and approach. I wish that many more scientists should follow the path shown by Professor Moharir and chronicle their experiences to enrich the present and the posterity.

I compliment and congratulate the author for his sterling contribution.

R. B. Singh
President
National Academy of Agricultural Sciences
New Delhi

July 27, 2013

Preface to the Second Edition

Ever since the publication of this book in 2013, all copies from the first printing were sold out within one and half year. It was published privately by me then as a result of repeated insistence and encouragement from my wife, who had seen me toil through my service career as a professional scientist. However, demand for copies of this book was gradually growing louder. Repeated printing of the book from new printing houses was difficult for quality reproduction. Still however, a soft copy of the book was posted by me on my personal profile page of 'Research Gate' website for professional scientists and researchers. Monitoring of the increasing readership of this book from this website convinced me that it is time to either go in for repeat printing of the book or to bring out a second revised and enlarged edition. I preferred the second option and therefore the provision of bringing out this edition of the book. I am happy that M/S Zorba Books, Gurugram, Haryana, India accepted my request to undertake the responsibility and publish it under their banner and I would like to thank Dr. Ms. Shalini Gupta and all members of the production team of Zorba Books for the help rendered in publication of the book.

The book was initially written in a 'free flowing style' as the ideas came to my mind without specifically planned headings and format. Whereas, the basic format and sequential order of the paragraphs has been retained as they were in the first edition, some of the paragraphs have been marginally revised and enlarged to some extent. Few pages on the post graduate school of IARI and basic frame-work of its working have been appended to provide readers, the idea about the kind of system and frame-work of conditions within which the author had spent his career. The description about all this pertains to the situation that existed between 1968 to until 2006-2010. And therefore the description and views expressed by me within pages of this book are purely my own. The IARI/ICAR authorities or organizations have nothing to do with my personal opinions kept and expressed by me as a participating insider. It is quite likely that situations may have changed for good within the institute ever since I wrote about them in 2013. I was fortunate to get the foreword for the first edition of this book from none other than Padma Bhushan Professor Ram Badan Singh, President, National Academy of Agricultural Sciences (NAAS), who had also been my Director at the Indian Agricultural Research Institute. I am equally fortunate now to get a foreword for the current edition, from Professor Vidya Bhushan (V. B.) Gupta, my own teacher and guru, a renowned polymer physicist, former Professor, Head of Department of Textile Technology and Dean of the Indian Institute of Technology, Delhi. Professor Gupta is currently heading the 'Distance Education Program' of the Dayalbagh Educational Institution *(Deemed University)* Agra. His commitment to the cause of education and seeking excellence in academic standards and stamina, even at his advanced age is exemplary. Moreover, as an individual, who has overseen my own career and journey, right from my studentship with him for my doctoral thesis and career at the IARI from 1975 to 2006 and even thereafter, there could not have been a more authoritative person to write a foreword for my 'professional autobiography' than him. What could have been more profound blessing for a student than this? I am grateful to Professor Gupta for so kindly agreeing to my request and do the needful.

As always, my wife and companion for over fifty years now, Mrs. Sulochana Anil Moharir and my daughter Mrs. Prachi Moharir Bajaj have both been a source of encouragement to keep me engaged in my creative work of writing popular articles on scientific subjects. I sincerely thank both of them tor all that they do for me. In the end, I hope that the present edition would be welcomed by the readers and particularly by the students and find this description of the struggle of a physicist in agricultural research informative and possibly encouraging too.

Anil Vishnu Moharir

Pune, Maharashtra

Preface to the First Edition

This book describes the struggle and challenges of a post graduate student in physics, fresh from a university and looking for opportunities to establishing himself in professional career and more for earning a livelihood. Shear accident or destiny *(if there is anything like that)* lands him in the national institute devoted to agricultural research without any learning, training or knowledge about biological cells, plants, genetics, soils or agriculture. The author as this student has described in his own characteristic style, how he steered himself, motivated by self confidence and in the learning he acquired as a post-graduate in physics, took roots and takes pride in whatever he contributed in the field of agricultural research. In unfolding this story, the author brings out the benefits of looking at his research problems from a multidisciplinary point of view and how his training in physics facilitated him to gain ground in an alien area such as agriculture. What has driven the author to write his account is his realization with conviction that the field of agriculture and biology is a goldmine for more and more innovative research in which trained physicists have a lot to contribute in cooperation with biologists. Whereas he appreciates the authorities who selected him and provided the opportunity in 1968 to work in a relatively unknown hybrid discipline of Agricultural Physics, he hopes that many new students from the discipline of physics will venture to enter and find challenging opportunities in the fields of biology and agriculture. Also, in turn, the authorities in the ICAR and State Agricultural Universities would open themselves to welcome physicists and realize that knowledge is a universal continuum and there should be an unrestricted flow of people from all specialty areas without fear, apprehensions, obstructions, restrictions, reservations and discriminations. The situation has changed considerably in last five decades and the authorities in the exclusive Agricultural Universities established in the country in particular would appreciate that major strides and innovative research can progress better and faster with strengthening the faculties of basic sciences. Like any old, conventional or new technology, it is hard to find a branch of agricultural science which does not contain or depends on some amount of physics in them. Agricultural universities should not isolate themselves to remain as the exclusive pastures for graduates and post graduates produced by them. The author admits that experience of working in an agricultural research institute has not only widened his mental faculties but has provided a comprehensive understanding of the material continuum in the universe that exists within the dimensions of **10^{28}** to **10^{-14} cm,** i.e. from the distant cosmos to size of elementary particles. Perhaps, this would not have been possible so easily otherwise. It has helped him to reach closer to realize the roots of our ancient 'Vedic' and 'Upanishad' philosophy and their continued relevance even today in a complementary way and not in opposition. The author was barely three years old when India became independent in 1947 and has grown and lived with the country since then. While narrating his story and experiences as a keen student of politics in India, Indian philosophy, history, culture and social sciences since childhood, has also analyzed and reflected on the situations, conditions then existed and implications of those policy decisions on life in general, working of institutions and in creating a congenial atmosphere for collective progress and development in the country from his own personal point of view. These observations, despite the risk of being considered by the readers as 'out of context' with reference to the title, are the logical extensions of thoughts in relation to the point under description. They are by no means meant to denigrate the contribution and importance of any individual or leader but only suggestive of some better option that could have been possible in the national interest. As an example, it may be worth quoting the experience described by the Japanese Prime Minister Mr. Yosuhiro Nakasone in their Parliament (Diet). After the end of World War-II, Japan adopted the American pattern of education in schools in preference over their traditional pattern of education and consciously introduced excessive competition at every stage of schooling in attempts to goad students to excel. The result of this policy decision more than five decades after its introduction was that Japan faced the problem of highest juvenile crimes in the world. Every student in Japan became psychologically more eager to eliminate his immediate competitor than to stay in healthy competition. In a democratic country, it is not always good to go by the number in arriving at a decision , sometimes the majority must bow to the opinion of the most enlightened, sagacious, experienced and foresighted individual from amongst them, It is only hoped that the readers of this booklet, despite disagreement, would look to the views of the author from this perspective in mind and certainly find this narration interesting, revealing, thought provoking, factual and worth retrospection. It is also believed that students in our agricultural and conventional universities and those already engaged in research in all scientific institutions irrespective of disciplines, would find the experiences described by the author interesting, stimulating and perhaps motivating.

I am indebted to Padma Bhushan Professor Ram Badan (R. B.) Singh, currently, President, National Academy of Agricultural Sciences and my Director at the Indian Agricultural Research Institute during my service period for so kindly agreeing to write the Foreword for this book. He is one of those few individuals who had impressed me most with not only with his scholarship, open mind, magnanimity at the heart and humility but with character as a fine and sensitive human being, No wonder, I feel deeply elated and honoured with his kind gesture. He had also been instrumental in providing me his experienced and sagacious advice in the compilation of my earlier book in felicitation of Professor A. B. Joshi, the greatest agricultural scientist of the post-independence era.

(Anil Vishnu Moharir)

Dated: October 14, 2013
New Delhi

1

Search for a Career Opportunity

A post-graduate student of physics would probably never intentionally imagine the kind of opportunities that may be lying for work in an area other than his field of specialization. Passion, loves for the subject, urge to grasp and master the techniques remain the prime considerations uppermost in his mind during such formative training as a physicist. I was certainly no exception to such a situation. Therefore, going in for a Doctorate Degree at the earliest, soon after the masters degree was my only goal and to my great delight, I was accepted by Professor V.G. Bhide, a renowned physicist to that end under his guidance. He even made me seriously initiate my work on preparing selenium photo-conductive cells from the middle of 1967, and allowing me to join his group at the National Physical Laboratory, pending formal registration in a university and arrangement of a suitable fellowship for me. However, destiny *(if there is anything like that?)* had some different designs for me and my career. Financial constraints and circumstances arising out of sudden deputation of Professor V.G. Bhide to USA for two years forced me to look for alternate option or career. By chance, my attention was drawn to an advertisement inviting applications from post-graduates in physics for research career in a hybrid discipline called 'Agricultural Physics' and this pushed me into little contemplation. I knew that the farthest distance that can be reached with the best of telescopes in space is $\mathbf{10^{28}}$ cm and the smallest that can be visualized with microscopic techniques being $\mathbf{10^{-14}}$ cm. What lies in between these two extreme limits of human knowledge is nothing but only matter *(both animate and inanimate)* and energies of various kinds and their interactions. As a trained physicist, I asked myself; Am I not trained to deal with matter and energies of various kinds and their mutual interactions? Am I not familiar with tools and techniques to study and unravel the nature, composition and structure of such matters? With this introspection and with an emphatic- 'YES' in affirmation to my questions, I decided to submit my application and even foray in the field of agriculture dealing principally with soils and plant biological materials, if selected. This was both a challenge and a risk that I had thrown to myself because I lacked the formal training, idea or any learning in the field of agriculture or biology. It was virtually like swimming in an ocean without a compass. Any frustration in the event of being unsuccessful later could have ruined me both mentally and psychologically. However, my confidence and faith in my training as a physicist helped me in resolutely overcoming all negative thoughts. Perhaps, the book 'Giants of Science' containing biographies of some of the greatest scientists that I had read seriously during my graduation, helped me in doing so. Every scientist I read about had the courage to tread an unknown path and faced innumerable difficulties in his / her life. Very soon, I received a call for a formal interview before the selection committee comprising of Dr. L. A. Ramdas, the celebrated, physicist, meteorologist and former Director General, India Meteorological Department, Dr. C. Dakshinamurti, the founder Head of the Division of Agricultural Physics and three others. My performance in the interview was good and selection was almost obvious from the fact that the chairman proposed to recommend and grant four advance increments in salary in the interview itself.

2

The First Step for a Research Career

Having made up my mind, I joined the Division of Agricultural Physics of the Indian Agricultural Research Institute as Senior Research Assistant in December 1968. During my introduction to the members of the staff of the Division, I realized that a good number of physicists were already there in position. They included besides Dr. C. Dakshinamurti, Professor Y. V. Kathavate, a spectroscopist and a student of Sir C. V. Raman (NL); Dr A. R. Deb, a biophysicist; Dr. S. C. Mehta, a radiological physicist; Dr. G. S. R. Krishnamurti, a wide-angle X-Ray diffraction specialist and soil-clay mineralogist; Mr. Nam Prakash, a particle physicist and transmission electron microscopist; Dr. V. A. K. Sarma a physical chemist; Dr. R. P. Gupta, a soil physicist and Mr. Bhagwat Khawas, a protein crystallographer. Dr B. C. Panda a small angle X-ray diffraction specialist; Mr. P. S. N. Sastry, and Dr. C. V. S. Sastry, both meteorologists joined the division soon after me. In the process of the expansion of the division to take care of the teaching of various courses developed, many more individuals from the area of geology, soil physics and meteorology joined the division and they included Mr. K. S. Sunder Sarma; N. V. K. Chakravarty; U. S. Victor; T. V. Rao; A. D. Mongia; R. C. Joshi and M. C. Jain. Some others from the field of agricultural sciences as Dr. Y. N. Rao, Gurcharan Singh, K. G. Choudhari and N. R. Dutta also found place in the new hybrid discipline. The Division of Agricultural Physics, founded in 1962, had soon become vibrant with activities of both scientists and students, crowded within a relatively small working space provided within the building of the Division of Soil Science and Agricultural Chemistry and a few more rooms scattered within the Divisions of Entomology and Genetics nearby. The Division at that time was equipped with large Hilger-Littrow recording Spectrometer, microdensitometer, colorimeters, UV-Visible range spectrophotometers, optical and polarized light microscopes, Philips X-ray diffractometer and Philips EM-100 Transmission Electron Microscope in addition to a well equipped meteorological observatory located in the middle of the experimental farm area of the institute as some of the basic facilities for research besides some ancillary farm equipments, tools and implements for field research. The Division also maintained a moderate sized electronics and mechanical workshop for fabricating small improvised equipments and gadgets for any innovation and to carry out repairs, maintenance of equipments and audio-visual projection systems from other divisions. Mr. R. P. Mittal, a brilliant innovator but not with high academic qualifications was in-charge of this workshop assisted by a dedicated technician Mr. Subhash Chander. Mr. Mittal, out of frustration soon left the institute and made a fortune in selling the state-of-the-art printing machines and equipments of German origin. The Division of Agricultural Physics also maintained a well equipped glass blowing unit for fabricating day to day needs of glass wares for experimental use under Mr. Bhagwan Das an expert glass blower, besides a full-fledged functional photography section, equipped with the then, modern cameras and film processing and printing equipments as a central institute facility under a renowned photographer of the country Mr. Hari Krishan (H. K.) Gorkha. I am mentioning these names here because unfortunately there is no systemic mechanism at the institute (IARI) or at the Divisional level to maintain historical record, leave aside documents, epoch making manuscripts or even photographs of individual scientists who worked and contributed significantly or in whatever best way they could do at the institute. It was a big consolation that every member of the Agricultural Physics Division was very cooperative, understanding, supportive and working almost like one family. That is the reason for the obligatory mention of them individually above.

Most of the earlier work prior to 1962, carried out by the so called 'Physics Unit' within the establishment of the Division of Agricultural Chemistry (Renamed as Division of Soil science and Agricultural Chemistry after 1970) was on the estimation of available micronutrient status of the soils of India, micronutrient supplementation in relation to crop requirement and crop yields using spectro-chemical techniques, known for their precision. This was obvious because the senior most members, Dr. C. Dakshinamurti **(Fig.1)** and his deputy Dr. Y. V. Kathavate **(Fig.2)** were both Spectroscopists by training.

Figure 1: Dr. D. K. Das, Dr. C. Dakshinamurti and Dr. A. V. Moharir

Figure 2: Dr. Y. V. Kathavate

Dr. G. S. R. Krishnamurti and his group was engaged in identification of clay minerals from the various types of predominant soils from the states of India, with an objective of preparing state wise and later a national 'soil clay-mineral map' for use in various practical agricultural applications and possible modification of the physical properties of soils for optimum crop yields. In such complementary efforts Dr. R. P. Gupta and his group was running an 'All India Coordinated Project Study on Soil-profile and Soil-structure' of different soil types in an attempt to prepare a comprehensive soil-map of the country and to define soil characteristics and behaviour in terms of basic soil physical parameters. Looking at both these and various other projects and their objectives, I observed my own outlook suddenly broadened and I began to think of every problem from a holistic national perspective i.e. its needs, requirements, possibilities, strategies for realization and priorities. This was to me a realization of the importance of working in a National Institute and associating with people with innovative Pan-Indian ideas, objectives and dreams. Everyone here was engrossed and inflamed with the passion for his own research work and sincere convictions to deliver results at the earliest.

3

My Exposure to the *De Facto* National Library on Agriculture at IARI

I was asked by Dr. G. S. R. Krishnamurti, under whom I was being groomed, to spend some time everyday in the institute library and read some specifically recommended books to get myself familiar with the broad aspects of the problems falling within the domain of an Agricultural Physicist. Moving through the huge stack rooms containing over six hundred thousand books and periodicals and large air-conditioned reading halls of the library, I could realize the wealth of this invaluable collection almost exclusively on all aspects of agriculture published from across the world. My head bowed in salute to all those who helped build this wonderful collection, not only for their own need but also for the posterity. It was a real pleasure and curious thrill to not only see but to read books published over two or three centuries before and in case of research problems, to go back to the very origin of the first thought published in print about it and pursue developments in the course of time. What was (and is) spectacular in respect of IARI library being the uninterrupted subscription of some of the best known research journals and their availability on the shelves? Visiting this wonderful 'open-access' library (*a rare privilege and honour, based on the confidence reposed in the integrity of the reader as a genuinely interested individual)* at IARI became my regular routine for at least four days in a week before returning home from the laboratory. At times, it was agonizing and appalling to find someone having torn or removed pages of important articles on new discoveries from the journals. Little did those responsible for such vandalism realized; what harm they were doing to the heritage for posterity. But they were those selfishly possessive and insensitive individuals who had been un-touched by intellectual influence and a chance to feel the warmth of disciplined manhood. By indulging in such vandalizing acts, they betrayed the faith, confidence, respect, dignity, honour and privilege that were given to them as a researcher / reader with a free open access to books, the invaluable heritage for posterity. Occasionally, I sincerely felt the pain and agony in bringing out such instances to the notice of the library authorities as they came to my attention during my reading schedules. Perhaps, it was a part of rigorous discipline enforced by my mother since childhood and the influence of having read many books by Dr. S. Ranganathan, on library science and management early in my student life, which my younger sister used to either purchase or borrow from her college library for her Bachelor of Library Science Degree she was pursuing. My regular visits to the IARI library made me a familiar figure and helped me build intimacy and friendship with all the senior and junior members of the library staff besides understanding on their problems, difficulties, frustration and limitations. In this context, the damage done by the ICAR authorities in shifting the post of the Chief Librarian from academic to the technical cadre and that too in the 'category of reserved positions' was most disturbing. The management, up-keep and regular up-dating of a *de-facto* National Library on Agriculture should not have been made a reserved pasture for a particular section of community. The name of this library has now been changed to 'Professor Dr. M. S. Swaminathan Library' in honour of Dr. M. S. Swaminathan. My extensive reading on all aspects of agricultural subjects provided me with a good comprehension in an integrated way. Perhaps, it was my training as a physicist that was following its logical gradient in seeking inter-disciplinary linkages and connections to problems. Later, in service, it was my pleasure to serve the cause of the library as a member of the institute library committee under the chairmanship of the Dean and Joint Director (Education).

4

My First Experience of Annual Convocation at IARI

The first major event I attended, in the process of getting introduced to the traditions in the institute, within three months of my joining, was the convocation week in February 1969. The Heads of various divisions presented the summary of major research achievements made during the preceding year from their respective disciplines and by students for their Ph.D. and M.Sc. degrees and during later years for competition for the various Gold Medals for best research theses. All Heads of Divisions in IARI that time were stalwarts and eminent scientists in their own right and their scientific presentations at the convocation, in fact were abject lessons for me in the art of presentation of scientific reports and public speaking besides providing a comprehensive understanding of research problems from a multidisciplinary angle. It was here I used to remember Mr. Guru Dayal Singh, my English language Teacher in school insisting on developing a command over the language of our expression and demanding us to write at least three pages on any fictitious topic everyday using at least five new words, possibly as adjectives, adverbs or verbs in describing the topic. He also used to repeatedly quote the quotation –*"Reading maketh a full man, conference a ready man and writing an exact man"* while encouraging us to write more and more. Mr. Guru Dayal Singh was equally gracious and prompt in returning the corrected pages of writing to students who took his advice seriously. I had taken to regularly write my everyday exercises in the form of long letters, addressed to my unknown friend in my diary. I think, I was deeply influenced in doing so by the book- 'The Diary of Anne Frank' which I had read in my childhood. The truth of what my teacher insisted was physically witnessed and experienced by me in the profoundly lucid lectures I heard on IARI campus. My own efforts in developing my expression since childhood stood in good stand with me when my Ph. D. supervisor Professor V. B. Gupta from the Indian Institute of Technology-Delhi **(Fig.3)** challenged me to reduce the original one hundred and seventy eight page draft of my Ph. D. theses into eighty pages including references.

Figure 3: Professor V. B. Gupta with A. V. Moharir (Left) in 1980

He even refused to sign the theses if it exceeded that limit. "What you described in so many pages can be said in even eighty pages," he said. With a goal set in the mind, to my surprise, I finished my final draft of the theses in just seventy nine pages without compromising objectivity and important details. This lesson, approach and attitude also helped me later in writing all my research papers forwarded to various journals both within and outside India. My convictions in developing command over language(s) was further boosted by Professor

Paul Kiekens, Director, Department of Textiles, State University of Ghent, during my visit to his laboratory in Belgium on a Fellowship from the Commission of European Communities. He advised me on the very first day in no uncertain terms and I quote verbatim- "Moharir -you are free to write and send any communication from this laboratory, but whatever you send for publication that bears the name of my laboratory, kindly ensure before hand that your manuscript is scientifically correct, technically sound, precisely brief and to the point in expression, grammatically perfect and free from typographical errors". There was abject lesson and profound message in these words. I am happy to record here that all the nine manuscripts I communicated from there were accepted for publication without editorial corrections, changes or suggestions from their reviewers. I could not have asked for a more profound compliment for my papers published in the Journal of Applied Polymer Science being described as 'very lucid' by none other than Dr. Atmaram Bhairav (A. B.) Joshi, the greatest agricultural scientist of modern India, who toiled and laid the foundation, to usher in, the first ever green revolution in the country **(Fig.4).**

Figure 4: Facsmile of the book-'Profile In Solitude'

5

The Lal Bahadur Shastri Memorial Lectures

From 1969, IARI introduced the annual lecture dedicated to the memory of the second Prime Minister of India, Late Shri Lal Bahadur Shastri, as a mark of tribute to his contribution to the nation, his recognition of the importance of Indian farmers to the prosperity and security of nation along with armed soldiers fighting on the border front of national boundaries. It was my privilege to have heard Shastriji delivering his famous slogan –'Jai Jawan Jai Kisan' during his address to the nation over radio in 1965, announcing Pakistani invasion on the Western border and India going in for a full-scale military war in defense of its territory. The inaugural 'Lal Bahadur Shastri Memorial Lecture of IARI was delivered by Dr. Vikram Ambalal Sarabhai, Chairman, Atomic Energy Commission & Indian Space Research Organization. In his eloquent speech, and elaborating over the early gains of the proverbial 'Green Revolution', Dr. Sarabhai pleaded for an active cooperation for Intensive Agricultural Development Programmes at the District level backed up by equally imaginative action involving the Centre and States cooperatively to stabilize and enhance the marginal gains achieved in agricultural production. He even cautioned that- "without an understanding of these matters, the green that we see would be like the green that suddenly appears on the landscape after the first showers in June, only to turn brown again when the monsoon is delayed". The 'Lal Bahadur Shastri Memorial Lectures' of IARI have since evolved into the most prestigious event, as an integral part of the institute convocation every year. For nearly 40 years hereafter, I enjoyed a rare privilege to physically see and to listen to some of the most talented minds, celebrated individuals, philosophers, thinkers, administrators, leaders and nation or institution builders delivering their brilliant Shastri Memorial speeches in their personal inimitable styles in the IARI convocations and on several other occasions. They included Dr. B. P. Pal; Dr. A. B. Joshi; Sir C. V. Raman (NL), B, Sivaraman; V. Kurien; V. Shankar; Dr. Ralph W. Cummings; Professor M. G. K. Menon; Professor M. S. Swaminathan; Professor A. S. Paintal; Dr. Norman E. Borlaug; Professor Satyen Bose (of Bose-Einstein Statistics fame); Dr. Ismail Serageldin; Justice M. Hidayatullah; Revered Mother Teresa (NL); Mr. T. N. Seshan; Dr. A. P. J. Abdul Kalam, Dr. R. A. Mashelkar and His Holiness Swami Nischalanand Saraswati, Shankaracharya of Goverdhan Peeth, Puri. The successive chain of towering leadership in IARI had always drawn and attracted eloquent speakers and well known scientists, scholars and philosophers from almost all the year around to the benefit of both staff and students. I do not think students in any other institution or a university in the country would be more fortunate to get so frequent opportunities to listen to such illustrious and eloquent speakers as in the IARI. Of course, it is up to an individual student or a scientist to either seize the opportunity for personal advantage or loose it. The pageant of first ever convocation, I attended at the IARI in 1969, the glamorous procession of the members of the Academic Council walking up to the dais in colourful gowns made a deep impression in my mind. No wonder, I should have nurtured a dream of proving myself worthy and becoming a part of this pageantry at some stage if I continued to be a part of the institute. It was a dream fulfilled, when I was appointed as the professor in the Division of Agricultural Physics later in my career. Also, I could not imagine that time that I would ever be invited by the Director-IARI to make an exclusive presentation on the life and contribution of Professor Atmaram Bhairav (A. B.) Joshi, the first Dean of the Post Graduate School of IARI during the Golden Jubilee Convocation of the Institute on February 07, 2008, immediately after the presentation of the prestigious Late Shri Lal Bahadur Shastri Memorial Lecture delivered by Dr. Subramaniam Nagarajan, Chairperson, Protection of Plant Varieties and Farmer's Rights Authority, Government of India. **Figure 5.**

Figure 5: A Memento presented by the Director-IARI to Dr. A. V. Moharir for making a special presentation on the life and work of Dr. A. B. Joshi, the first Dean of IARI-Post Graduate School at the Golden Jubilee Convocation on February 07, 2008.

6

Sir C. V. Raman and His Theory on Colours of Flowers

The memory of perhaps the last public lecture delivered by Sir C. V. Raman (NL) at the IARI (Held in the Auditorium of the National Physical Laboratory) in 1970, before he passed away is still fresh in my mind. Professor Raman, speaking on the subject –'Colours of Flowers', proudly displayed two separate flasks containing acetone extracts of two pigments he had isolated from flowers which he called them as 'Florachrome-A' and 'Florachrome-B'. Professor Raman further went on to state that the two extracts A & B mixed in different proportions, produce flowers of almost any colour. As a trained physicist, Raman's lecture had a deep influence on me and continued work as I thought at that time, on this subject would have been an ideal research project of considerable promise for a new entrant in the field of Agricultural Physics. This would have been easy to pursue and possibly provided an opportunity to explore its inter-disciplinary linkages to genetics, physiology, biochemistry of plant metabolic activity, species or environment in the origin and syntheses of colours of flowers in association with the scientists from the Division of Floriculture. Scientists here were already working on breeding of a host of flowers, particularly roses, gladiolas, bougainvillea and marigold for almost all seasons and work on the physics of colours of flowers would have made an important contribution. I lost no time in initiating preliminary discussions on the proposal and identify the willing collaborators. But unfortunately, the newly framed and imposed guidelines for scientists collaborating in number of divisional and inter-divisional research projects both as leader and associate worked more as deterrent for interdisciplinary collaborative work. The Research Project Form-I (RPF-I) evolved as a prelude to the newly proposed Agricultural Research Service Scheme *(formally launched on October 2, 1975)* evoked commitment on specified time allocation for all individual projects from scientists. It was merely an exercise of putting figures without any objective mechanism in place for accounting the exact time required for execution of the quantum of work committed. Despite this, nobody was prepared to take risk and get mired into official administrative controversies by exceeding limits of the number of projects for work and quantum of time committed in numerical figures.

Such procedures, policies and administratively binding actions were further compounded by the scary, non-scientist work auditors, virtually killing the enthusiasm, willingness for cooperation and initiatives for working on challenging ideas and freedom on the part of the scientists. How ridiculous were the RPF-I, II and III system, put into operation can be gauged from the fact that there were at one time, as many as 346 Research Projects in the institute duly approved by the Institute Research Council and the total budget required to operate all these approved projects from RPF-I figures was almost 200 times the actual budget of the institute. And all this followed from the inconvenient questions asked to scientists during the interviews for assessments and promotions to next cadres, when not being an independent research project investigator (PI) was considered to mean that the candidate scientist lacked leadership quality. Such questions and attitude promoted a culture and craving for individual project leadership amongst scientists and discouraged the spirit of cooperative group activity around scholar and scientifically meritorious leaders for resolving any research problem. There was no insistence on the part of authorities even to submit final RPF-III closing Project Report in ready to publish condition as a credit to both the institute and the concerned scientist, besides earning revenue from the sale of these published reports. Subsequent events changed my own course of work, priorities and I lost an opportunity in initiating work on ‘physics of the colours of flowers’ for ever. This work could have lasted for several years considering the enormity of the kind of flowers available, facilities for producing radiation induced mutations and a possible opportunity for identifying at least some common mechanism or principal determinants of the origin of colours in flowers. I still sincerely feel that some one in the Division of Agricultural Physics should pursue this subject in future. There is great promise in this study.

7

Proximity to the National Physical Laboratory

I consider myself fortunate as the National Physical Laboratory of India (NPL) from where I had started my career in 1967-68 was located within the IARI campus itself. As a result of my continued association and interactions with scientists there, I regularly received invitations from NPL for their 'Dr. K. S. Krishnan Memorial Lectures' in the memory of the first director Dr. K. S. Krishnan, FRS **(Figure 6).** These invitations provided me with my most cherished opportunities for over two decades to physically meet, interact, collect autographs *(as my hobby since childhood)* and listen to a large number of Nobel Laureates and pioneer scientists as speakers. Memories of lectures delivered in the NPL and my interactions with Prof. D. S. Kothari FRS, Prof. S. Chandrasekhar (NL), Madam Professor Dorothy Hodgkin (NL), Dr. David Shoenberg (NL), Professor Charles Townes (NL), Professor Ilya Prigogine (NL), Prof. C. N. R. Rao, FRS and many others are still fresh in my mind.

Figure 6: Professor Subramanyan Chandrashekhar (Nobel Laureate) signing my autograph book at the National Physical Laboratory after presenting the Dr. K. S. Krishnan memorial lecture

My association and collaboration with scientists from the NPL helped me in attending two International Schools organized there on; (1) International School in Synthesis, Crystal Growth and Characterization of Materials for Energy Conversion and Storage, held in October 1981 and (2) Indo-France School in Electron Microscopy in Material Science held in January 1990. These schools not only provided me with opportunity to interact with the French Scientist Dr. B. Jouffrey, a pioneer in High Voltage Transmission Electron Microscopy but theoretical and practical aspects of the science and art of Electron Microscopy and interpretation of the micro-world. Later my collaboration with Drs. D. K. Suri and K. C. Nagpal from the NPL helped me in using their instrumental facilities and producing some of my significant and widely cited research contribution on X-Ray diffraction and structure-property relationships in native cotton fibres on all the four commercial species of cotton, maintain my identity as a physicist and yet carry out research on problems of importance in agriculture. My proposed collaborative work on X-Ray topographical and micro-focus X-ray diffraction work on single developing and mature cotton fibres with Dr. Krishan Lal to unravel the mystery of the most enigmatic 'structural reversal bands' **(Fig.7)** observed along the length of cotton fibres under crossed polarized light in an optical microscope, to settle the issue of the physical disposition of micro-fibrillar cellulose within the matrix of secondary growth layers of cotton fibre at the positions where the bands appear.

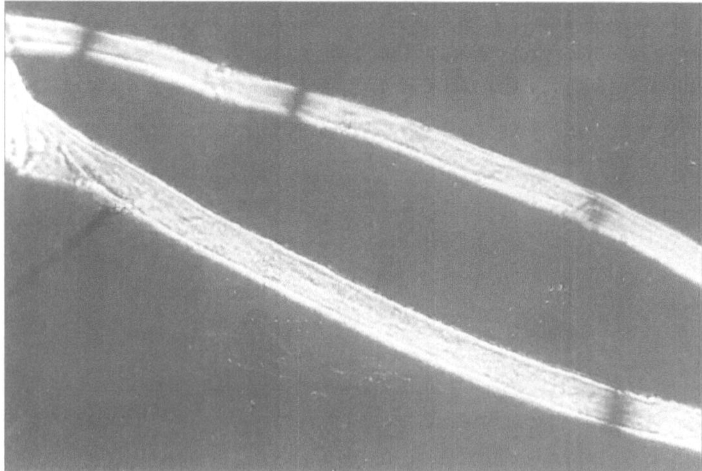

Figure 7: Reversal Bands along length of cotton fibres in crossed polarized light

This work was also expected to settle the long standing issue of these reversal bands being genetic or environmental in origin and whether they actually arise out of cellulose fibrils abruptly reversing their sense of spiral orientation at these points as first proposed by W. L. Balls in 1932 and believed since then. Following the nomenclature proposed by W. L. Balls, the dark bands along the length of cotton fibres observed in crossed-polarized light are therefore called 'reversals'. The locations of reversal bands along length of cotton fibres are being considered by some workers as weak points along which cotton fibres preferentially break during technological processing and as strong points by many others and there was no unanimity over this aspect. Application of high-resolution transmission electron microscope after its commercial availability in 1939 to study the structure of cotton fibres however, did not show any indication of cellulose fibrils reversing sense of orientation in ultrasonically broken and enzymetically degraded fragments of secondary layers of cotton. Only parallel disposition of micro-fibrils were seen. The possibility of reversal bands arising due to phase difference in the spiral disposition of bi-refringent *(crystalline materials having different refractive index values in mutually perpendicular directions)* crystalline cellulose micro-fibrils forming a cross oriented crystalline matrix between two or more successive secondary layers, as explained by me earlier in a published paper, could have been irrefutably worked out using X-Ray topography facilities at the NPL. The very idea though appreciated by the concerned scientists and despite their willingness to work together, actually got slaughtered at the altar of the crazy policy of commercialization adopted and pursued in scientific research and development organizations for charging and earning money for services, collaboration and instrumental facilities extended. Such a restrictive policy though justifiable on economic grounds was not conducive to creating new scientific knowledge through willing collaborations and sustained academic interests of scientists. Excessive commercialization of academic and research institutions breeds unhealthy competition leading to several undesirable practices, besides losing sight of public good at large as the prime motive of conducting research. However, I have always felt that despite sharing a common campus, the National Physical Laboratory and the Indian Agricultural Research Institute are not working together more often as they should do, on complementary programmes? Agricultural Sciences would always gain a lot from collaboration with physicists because physics, its laws and principles are the undercurrents of all material creations *(both animate and inanimate)* and fundamentals of disciplines including biology, medicine and agriculture.

8

Agricultural Physics in Retrospect

The influence of soil, climatic and weather conditions on vegetation and agricultural crop plants had been known to mankind since time immemorial. In fact the various crop cultivation practices evolved in various parts of the world are direct consequences of such observations, realizations and intelligent incorporation of strategies for maximization of crop yields based on the crop plant behaviours. However, Professor E. Wollny in Germany was the first to have mooted and evolved initial concepts of Agricultural Physics as an integrated subject and even published the 'Journal of Agricultural Physics' regularly from 1877 to 1898. Professor Franklin Hiram (F. H.) King at the University of Wisconsin in the Unites States of America actually held the position of Professor of Agricultural Physics as far back as from 1888 to 1902 and had made some fundamental contribution in the application of physics to agriculture, largely in the area of soil physics, water-holding capacities, water requirement of plants, soil aeration and movement of water in soils and under ground, draft of ploughs and several other cases. Professor F.H. King published his celebrated books 'Physics of Agriculture' in 1901 and 'Farmers of Forty Centuries' in 1911, and therefore Professor King is rightfully recognized as the father of Soil Physics. A Japanese Physicist is also reported to had published a book in 1905, entitled-'Agricultural Physics' hybridizing disciplines of physics, plant-biology, chemistry and meteorology together and their applications in agriculture. Further, G. Schubler in 1838 in Germany is credited with the first ever-systematic study of the physical and chemical properties of soils. Other excellent texts such as 'Soil Physics' by L. D. Baver, published in 1940 and 1948; 'Agricultural Physics' by C. W. Rose (1966) and 'Advanced Soil Physics' by Don Kirkham and W. L. Powers (1972) have put the subject of Agricultural Physics on sound scientific foundations for continued relevance as an essential part of the curriculum in agricultural sciences.

9

Some Policy Issues that Bothered, Intrigued and Disturbed Me

India, one of the oldest countries on the earth with a recorded history of flourishing agrarian civilization from 8000 BC, has a wealth of wisdom written and preserved on the practice of agriculture, animal husbandry, weather, seasons and rotational cycles of cereal crops, suitable for native conditions in ancient texts. There are even vivid descriptions of the positions of planets and heavenly constellations on the cycles of seasons on earth, their impacts on human psychology, physiology, and consequences of the type of food consumed during different seasons, remedies and incidences of pests and diseases that proliferate in these seasons. Even today, our calendar *(Panchang)* makers are predicting prospects of monsoon at least a year and half in advance based on the planetary positions and configurations of the celestial Zodiacal constellations. These predictions, as I have been consciously observing for years, are almost equally accurate with same levels of probability as are being given out by the India Meteorological Department on the basis of computer simulated models barely a few months in advance of the onset of monsoon every year. Reasonably accurate predictions based on astrological parameters about monsoon was being regularly made until recently by Mr. Dhansukhlal Shah from Gujrat for years. These reasonably accurate predictions can never happen as a matter of shear coincidence on perpetual basis and our present generation of scientists must at least attempt to search those hidden or unknown cosmological parameters, related scientific logic or theory and reasons for continued correlations of these predictions and actual incidental occurrence over the years. My own colleague Dr. K. S. Sunder Sarma, a geologist by training and practicing soil physicist, who was very good in such astronomical / astrological calculations and even at predictive astrology, could have easily applied his mind in this direction, as I personally feel, to discover such correlations in scientific ways. He was in a very advantageous position with respect of meteorological data for several decades in the past being available within the Division itself. Perhaps, the mindset in general to consider such studies being unscientific might have prevented him from making such an attempt. However, there seems no virtue in shying away from such studies at least now, in view of the current knowledge gained from several studies conducted by NASA from space-borne satellites and inner-planetary probes that the entire solar system is intimately inter-connected and there is a continual exchange of energies between the constellations, galaxies and planets of our own solar system. The role of so called 'subtle energies' though not yet identified and clearly documented by the physicists but their existence is inferred from indirect evidences, can also be examined for possible connection. One such example being the connection between the cosmic ray intensities, cloud formation, global warming and cycles of ice-ages on the Earth, experimentally demonstrated by Henrik Svensmark and his colleagues from Denmark ***(References 1-8).*** The very fact that every thing material that exists in the universe is made of atoms formed within furnaces of exploding stars and the component constituent particles of those individual atoms on their part being made up from the elementary particles called the 'quarks' have been linked together through a chain of successive events explained by the 'Standard Model of Atomic Structure' which attempts to combine all the four fundamental forces of nature; weak interaction, strong interaction, electromagnetic and gravitation under one common dream theory, for which, Albert Einstein spent the last three decades of his life without personal success but paving the path for others to follow. There are therefore, no barriers between disciplines. Knowledge is but one continuum and it is we, who unnecessarily draw and bind ourselves within limited boundaries. It is my opinion and conviction that a true scientist should enjoy absolute freedom to express his creativity, fearlessly transgress and intermingle across borders of disciplines to seek correlated relationships for exploring the truth. I do not mean to suggest that students or scientists need to become expert in all areas but they must train and equip themselves with a foundational understanding of areas that enable communication and comprehension among experts in various disciplines possible. And as Sir William Lawrence Bragg (NL) said- "The important thing in science is not so much to obtain new facts as to discover new ways of thinking about them" because the sole purpose and aim of science is to do honour to the human spirit. An amazing example of how interdisciplinary knowledge of meteorology, climatology, astronomy, astronomical climatology, geology, geography, medical sciences, human psychology and Sanskrit language can be used to accurately work out the exact dates of births of Shri Ram *(Chaitra Shuddha Navami, corresponding to 4 th December 7323 BC)*, Shrikrishna *(Shravan Krishna Ashtami, corresponding to 23rd May 5626 BC)* and the various other important incidences mentioned in the Ramayana and Mahabharata Epics and the Vedas from the accurately recorded positions of the heavely constellations, months and dates *(Teethis)* according to the Indian Lunar calendar for those events corresponding to the continuing Gregorian Calendar *(interpolated in retrospect)* being used these days, has been demonstrated by Late Bramharshi Dr. Padmakar Vishnu Vartak with evidences that both Shri Ram and Shrikrishna and other individuals who figure in both these epics were indeed historical persons ***(References 9,10)***.

Unfortunately, compulsions and obsession with Western education, materialistic deductive science and European languages in which much of the modern original scientific research and discoveries were being published, the prestige, prominence and monetary advantage they enjoyed for some obvious economic reasons have relegated study, understanding and practice of our own ancient science *(The Upanishads*), educational and medicinal systems and languages to a great extent into oblivion. The reasons for this state of affairs are many but the most significant being the neglect of promoting literacy and education through almost thirteen hundred years of slavery ever since the Muslim invaders (712 AD) started taking control of the erstwhile princely states in India and systematically took to destroying the traditional values, educational and cultural systems and symbols in the country. The British, who followed the Mughals until 1947 AD, in attempts to consolidate their political power, promoted, encouraged and even forced sycophancy, sabotage, bribery, subversion, treachery and patronized conversion to Islamic and Christian *(Both having a common origin)* faiths as easy virtues under extreme economic poverty, illiteracy, unemployment and lack of other opportunities for survival. Social discriminations between various castes and family boycott of progressive social reformers from upper-castes, enforced by the stubborn and rigid priests of the Hindu communities for non-compliance and non-observing insensible, rigorous, ritualistic practices based purely on blind faith, ordinarily beyond economic means of people also contributed to their desperately accepting conversions than to suffer perpetual humiliation and social boycott. Progressive social reformers even wanted to accept and bring back converted Hindus to the faith of their birth at a penance but the rigid priests did not budge and permit re-conversions to original faith. In fact, the stubborn Hindu priests who wielded considerable influence and authority in society and their blind followers divided the Hindu community much more than what the invaders could have possibly done on their own. The Muslim invaders and later the British merely took advantage of the weaknesses of mindset and already existing divide amongst the Hindus based on incorrect and often intentionally mischievous, partisan and selfish interpretation of 'Brahmanical Texts' and divided loyalties to the erstwhile rulers, to consolidate their control over the governance of the Indian sub-continent.

After the independence in 1947, the nation should have been put on a corrective course by reverting back and adoption of our traditional value based education, philosophy, principles, policies for quality governance and administration sans social and communal discrimination as guiding foundations of state policies but despite massive electoral mandate behind himself, it was not done so by Pandit Jawaharlal Nehru *(who was formally educated in England since childhood)* the first Prime Minister and Mr. Maulana Abul Kalam Azad, first education minister of the government of independent India. It is still a mystery for me, why the successive congress governments at the centre, preferably appointed ministers for education from only the Muslim community. There appears to be, more a design in this action than a mere coincidence, particularly when there was no dearth of impartial erudite scholars and intellectuals from the majority Hindu community in the country. The results of these appointments have since been seen in a systematic gradual and clandestine distortion of the factual history of the Mughals in India and denigration of the Hindu

Kings and Rulers, through the National Council of Educational Research and Training (NCERT) syllabi and text-books, meant for distribution in schools in the country. Still however, they were instrumental in creating new institutions in the country such as the University Grants Commission; chain of the Indian Institutes of Technology; the Indian Institute of Science; Council of Scientific and Industrial Research and laboratories; the Lalit Kala and Sangeet Natak Academies and many more. We adopted westernized model of parliamentary democracy and constitution besides accepting continued retention of the administrative format of judicial and civil service rules framed by the British for their convenience and rule. No wonder, the old rules and regulations do not match the new aspirations of free democratic India. For decades after independence, instead of vigorous promotion of literacy, education, agriculture and rural development in preference to rapid industrialization, budget allocation for education was less than 1% of GNP. Agriculture was grossly neglected with the result that our Food and Agriculture Ministers were going around the world for years, begging for food-grains until the situation was saved by the introduction of Dr. Norman E. Borlaug's high yielding, nitrogenous-fertilizer-responsive, Mexican dwarf wheat varieties in the fertile farm soils of the Gangetic plain. Now, for nearly five decades since then, India has enjoyed a comfortable situation in respect of food grains. However, excessive indiscriminate application of synthetic nitrogenous chemical fertilizer, agro-chemicals *(insecticides, pesticides, herbicides and weedicides, growth promoting hormones)* and tube-well irrigation has not only turned thousands of hectares of fertile farm land in Punjab, Haryana, Uttar Pradesh and Rajasthan into highly saline unproductive wastelands but has also led to excessive pollution of rivers, wells and ground water aquifers. Population of once healthy villages in the above mentioned states are rapidly turning into communities of cancer patients besides pushing the country as whole on the brink of ecological disaster. On an average, 18 persons are dying everyday due to cancer in the Faridkot district of Punjab alone and the situation is worsening in other areas as crop-years pass by. The severe implications of large-scale annual withdrawal of gaseous Nitrogen from the atmosphere in ever increasing quantities for manufacture of fertilizers and industrial applications on human health, ecosystem and in global warming has been recently reviewed by me ***(Reference 11).*** This is the first ever report that talks about the consequences of such annual withdrawal of atmospheric nitrogen on massive scale to be more serious than marginal increase or decrease of the other green house gases *(Carbon dioxide, Carbon monoxide, Methane, Ozone, Water vapours etc.)* being discussed regularly in national or international conferences. Despite these, I am afraid; no government from the developing countries would dare to reduce their consumption of nitrogenous fertilizer and risk even marginal losses in production of food grains for political and economic stability.

The government in more than six decades since independence has not been able to even implement free compulsory primary education to children without gender bias despite constitutional guarantee and obligation. Such failures in fulfilling constitutionally obligatory promises and meeting targeted goals, compromising the sanctity of the spirit of the constitution on the part of state and central governments have now almost become routine. The reasons may be many but in my personal opinion, the Constitution we have given to ourselves, modeled on the British pattern of democracy and more particularly the way it has been so frequently and indiscriminately amended and practically worked in the last seven decades since 1952, has proved to be more disintegrative than unifying in promoting the spirit of common and collective nationality, culture of inter-state cooperation and competition in scientific and technological development, sharing natural resources and promoting public and private investments in joint ventures between states from local resources. The governments of different political parties operating in the states, though outwardly working smooth are at times opposed to policies of the central government. The central government has also on occasions acted in unconstitutionally partisan and treacherous ways in toppling popularly elected state governments. This has unnecessarily incited media-wars, rivalries, violent demonstrations, rebellions, bitterness between states and migration of population to different states in search of employment and livelihood. Neither the Central Government nor the Parliament has been able to evolve any effective mechanism to enforce and ensure at least uniform minimum economic progress, development and quality of life and services in constituent states. The root cause of migration of people between states being; rising cost of living and spiraling inflation, lack of progressive, dedicated, committed and foresighted leadership, lack of economic and infrastructure development, illiteracy, religious orthodoxy, emotional exploitation, superstitions, excessive importance to observing ritualistic practices and blind faith of people, poor quality of roads and transport services, schools, colleges and university education and no opportunities for livelihood. No wonder, the judiciary has to frequently intervene in correcting governmental decisions and actions. Most of the national earnings today are being spent in maintaining our costliest constitutional parliamentary and legislative structure, institutions and disbursement of facilities, benefits and perks to legislators and in political maneuvering for power and positions rather than on economic development and progress. Even funds allocated for mitigating social inequalities are not reaching the needy because of excessive corruption at all levels of administrative and political structure. The constitutional framework and positions have become the legalized means for collective loot by the politicians enjoying immunity against judicial prosecution in the absence of impartial, independent investigating agencies and more because of the compulsions of sharing political power under politics of coalitions both at the centre and at state levels. The out of phase elections, engineered in one state or the other has further complicated our political system and economic priorities. Above all, despite the fact that the Indian Constitution was drafted and framed by the specially constituted 'Constituent Assembly' consisting of 300 members, the treacherous politicians projected one single individual as the sole architect of the Indian constitution, spreading incorrect information, gross misunderstanding, misconceptions besides undermining the role played by other eminent and illustrious members of the assembly involved in drafting the integrated document- 'The Constitution of India'. All this, paved the way for a nationally divisive 'vote-bank' politics and emergence of self-seeking, sectional mafia groups in the name of 'Regional Political Parties' and splintered break-away groups of disgruntled individuals from large National parties. When the best of stable democratic nations in the world are running institutions and affairs of their countries with only two political parties contesting elections for political power, it is amazing why in India we cannot do so? Why do we still prefer to divide our precious 'Votes' among several contestants and declare one with less than 10% share of total electorate as the winner and our representative in legislative assemblies or parliament? There is tremendous need for convictions, sincerity, genuine nationalist concern and political will for introducing drastic electoral reforms and generating public awareness for national good.

There are very few authoritative studies on initial formulation of educational and science policy ***(Figure.8, a, b, c)*** issues of the post independence period except critical post-facto, post-mortem reports on the decisions implemented.

GOVERNMENT OF INDIA

SCIENTIFIC POLICY RESOLUTION

NEW DELHI

Dated the 4th March, 1958 / 13th Phalguna 1879

Reprint for Department of Science & Technology by INSDOC, New Delhi-110012.

GOVERNMENT OF INDIA

SCIENTIFIC POLICY RESOLUTION

New Delhi, the 4th March 1958/13*th Phalguna*, 1879

No. 131/CF/57.—The key to national prosperity, apart from the spirit of the people, lies, in the modern age, in the effective combination of three factors, technology, raw materials and capital, of which the first is perhaps the most important, since the creation and adoption of new scientific techniques can, in fact, make up for a deficiency in natural resources, and reduce the demands on capital. But technology can only grow out of the study of science and its applications.

2. The dominating feature of the contemporary world is the intense cultivation of science on a large scale, and its application to meet a country's requirements. It is this, which, for the first time in man's history, has given to the common man in countries advanced in science, a standard of living and social and cultural amenities, which were once confined to a very small privileged minority of the population. Science has led to the growth and diffusion of culture to an extent never possible before. It has not only radically altered man's material environment, but, what is of still deeper significance, it has provided new tools of thought and has extended man's mental horizon. It has thus influenced even the basic values of life, and given to civilization a new vitality and a new dynamism.

3. It is only through the scientific approach and method and the use of scientific knowledge that reasonable material and cultural amenities and services can be provided for every member of the community, and it is out of a recognition of this possibility that the idea of a welfare state has grown. It is characteristic of the present world that the progress towards the practical realisation of a welfare state differs widely from country to country in direct relation to the extent of industrialisation and the effort and resources applied in the pursuit of science.

4. The wealth and prosperity of a nation depend on the effective utilisation of its human and material resources through industrialisation. The use of human material for industrialisation demands its education in science and training in technical skills. Industry opens up possibilities of greater fulfilment for the individual. India's enormous resources of man-power can only become an asset in the modern world when trained and educated.

5. Science and technology can make up for deficiencies in raw materials by providing substitutes, or, indeed, by providing skills which can be exported in return for raw materials. In industrialising a

2

country, a heavy price has to be paid in importing science and technology in the form of plant and machinery, highly paid personnel and technical consultants. An early and large scale development of science and technology in the country could therefore greatly reduce the drain on capital during the early and critical stages of industrialisation.

6. Science has developed at an ever-increasing pace since the beginning of the century, so that the gap between the advanced and backward countries has widened more and more. It is only by adopting the most vigorous measures and by putting forward our utmost effort into the development of science that we can bridge the gap. It is an inherent obligation of a great country like India, with its traditions of scholarship and original thinking and its great cultural heritage, to participate fully in the march of science, which is probably mankind's greatest enterprise today.

7. The Government of India have accordingly decided that the aims of their scientific policy will be–

(i) to foster, promote, and sustain, by all appropriate means, the cultivation of science, and scientific research in all its aspects–pure, applied, and educational;

(ii) to ensure an adequate supply, within the country, of research scientists of the highest quality, and to recognize their work as an important component of the strength of the nation;

(iii) to encourage, and initiate, with all possible speed, programmes for the training of scientific and technical personnel, on a scale adequate to fulfil the country's needs in science and education, agriculture and industry, and defence;

(iv) to ensure that the creative talent of men and women is encouraged and finds full scope in scientific activity;

(v) to encourage individual initiative for the acquisition and dissemination of knowledge, and for the discovery of new knowledge, in an atmosphere of academic freedom;

(vi) and, in general, to secure for the people of the country all the benefits that can accrue from the acquisition and application of scientific knowledge.

The Government of India have decided to pursue and accomplish these aims by offering good conditions of service to scientists and according them an honoured position, by associating scientists with the formulation of policies, and by taking such other measures as may be deemed necessary from time to time.

GIPND—DME—128 C.S.—21-3-58—2.000

Figure 8 (a, b, c): Science policy document of Government of India

An excellent critical review of the overall policies framed and pursued by Pt. Jawaharlal Nehru for seventeen long years as the first Prime Minister and the cult of hero-worship that came into cultivation has been written by Mr. N. R. Waradpande in his book-'Nemesis of Nehru Worship" ***(Reference 12).***

Partition of India was an unfortunate decision thrust upon the country by the Muslim League, the Congress and the British government. However, despite accepting the partition of the country on the basis of religion, a large section of Muslim *(Converts from the Hindu faith under fear or compulsions of some kinds)* population opted to stay back *(either intentionally or under design and cover of some kind of long-term hidden agenda)* and refused to migrate to the new theocratic nation of Pakistan *(Divided then between two parts the East and West parts)* for reasons of common heritage, ancestry, culture and mutual blood-relationships. No wonder, with blood-relatives spread across borders, the post-independence leaders in Pakistan, in attempts to provide and infuse a separate identity and nationality in the minds of people, should have deliberately followed and spread the 'Hate India' campaigns and policies in East and West Pakistan. It was traumatic even for the Indian Muslims across border to reconcile to a sudden change of their nationality overnight. As a fall out of the policies and actions taken by Pakistan and feelings of insecurity aroused, the Muslim population which opted to stay back in India changed the course of polity, quality of governance with the so called new democratic rulers adopting and resorting to exciting, appeasement, reservations and vote-bank politics as means to share political power. The continued retention of both Hindu and Muslim personal laws, as I personally see, is a national tragedy. It is my personal sincere conviction that Hindus as a community have also failed to project, profess, practice, observe and communicate the profound teachings of Vedas, Upanishads and Gita, as Universal philosophies of their convictions for mutual and collective existence and more as 'scientific treatises' as they actually are and not the religious texts. The science of our physical, physiological, mental, psychological and social existence on the Earth, and the survival strategies under varying natural circumstances as the 'true religion' described in these ancient books is not only relevant in the twenty first century today but cuts universally across all religious faiths and geographical continents. Unfortunately, scientists in India do not bother to learn Sanskrit language for themselves and look at our ancient Sanskrit texts from scientific angle and contents. On the other hand, the so called Sanskrit language scholars do not comprehend and understand the hard-core science described in them. Today as I stand at the fag end of my life, I realize and regret for not having learnt Sanskrit language since childhood. The combination groups of subjects for Higher Secondary examination and graduation at universities set and forced on students by the authorities offered no scope for study of extra-optional subjects with credits. In my own house, I had an exemplary example of my maternal uncle Dr. R. J. Kalamkar, a renowned agricultural scientist and first Ph. D. student of the legendary statistician Professor R. A. Fisher, frustrated for not having learnt Sanskrit as a student of science, willfully completed his graduation (B. A.) and first year of Post Graduation (M. A.) in Sanskrit, with determination at the age of 65 years, long after his retirement from service. After my retirement from service in 2006, I did enroll myself with the 'Rashtriya Sanskrit Sansthan' for preliminary course in Sanskrit language through postal lessons. Unfortunately, my lessons never reached me in time and in proper serial sequenctial order. Frustration gripped me more than anything else and I discontinued my lessons. Perhaps I lacked the kind of determination, mental capacity for retention and ability to memorize words to follow my maternal uncle. But I have willfully studied with deep interest the authoritatively written commentaries on our ancient texts-Vedas, Upanishads and Gita in Marathi and I sincerely wish, unlike innumerable conventionally routine, stale, emotionally coloured with blind faith and incorrectly interpreted commentaries available in the market, the authoritative scientific exposition and interpretation of the 'Upanishads' 'Vedas' and the 'Gita' done by renowned Sanskrit scholar and practicing modern professional scientist Dr. P. V. Vartak and Dr. M. R. Guney ***(References 13, 14)*** should be translated and distributed widely amongst our scientist fraternity and young generation. Let our scientists and young generation realize, what modern science is searching and elaborating today about the truth and cause of the creation in nature was already known to the Indian Sages about 10,000 or more years before the Christian Era (BC). We lost connection to our ancient wisdom and knowledge because we lost our esteem and honour and neglected our mother tongue-Sanskrit. Instead of practically following the teachings of these ancient texts in behavior and actions, we merely reduced them to objects of physical worship and rituals in temples and at homes. The climax of all these was to put copies of 'Gita' in the courts for taking hypo critic oath for speaking the truth and yet giving false evidences and conveniently deceive. However, I am still of the opinion that despite record of scientific achievements by the ancient Indian Sages, the contribution of the Western world in developing logic and reason for subjecting scientific ideas and thoughts to 'practical experimental verification' on mathematical theories, developing applications and mass industrial production of materialistic scientific devices for large-scale consumption in society cannot be denied. However, despite these developments, the modern economic socialism attempted through scientific and industrial revolution has failed to curb jealousies, hatrade, greed, superstitions, blind faith in ritualistic traditional religious practices, racial discrimination and control the human mind. On the contrary, the Indian Sages invoked people to go individually within the human body and personally discover for themselves, the truth of creation and source of mental peace. The emotional excitement being aroused about fanatic practice of Islam religion and systematic brainwashing of young minds in Pakistan against India with group after group of perverted individuals offering them for perpetrating violence and killing of innocent people, clearly indicate the conditioning of minds and thoughts are more influential than subtle bonds of common inheritance and blood relationships. It is in situations like this, we realize the cardinal importance of the teachings for controlling mind and thoughts by the 'Vedas', Upanishads' and 'Gita' because all physical human actions, cruel or compassionate, stem from the thoughts in our mind.

10

Reorganization of States in India on Linguistic Basis and its Implications for Quality of Research and Education

After the independence in 1947, the boundaries of various states were redrawn on the basis of linguistic majority with a promise to promote and bring all Indian languages literally, scientifically and technically at par with other languages in the progressive world. The three language formula comprising of compulsory teaching of regional State language / Mother tongue, Hindi and English in schools uniformly in all states was adopted to meet the essential needs of a growing child and his aspirations in future as a civilized sovereign national or global citizen. This was a very good 'middle path' for a newly independent nation with complexities of diverse cultures and languages. Despite political opposition to teaching Hindi in the southern states, I trust that a young child is very quick in picking up languages through association and implementation of the three language formula would not have been a burden on a growing child. Alas, this was not to be. Riots were politically incited in the name of languages and what we have actually achieved in realty through all these post-independence years needs no elaboration and is familiar to every one. It is rare to find an individual from any linguistic States in the country who can speak fluently in chaste State-language without either mixing words from different languages or sentences or abruptly switching over to English during conversations. There is not one state that can boast of up-to-date facilities or institutions to conduct and publish research in science, engineering, technology and medical or sciences in local state language? Is this all we wanted to achieve by carving out states on the basis of languages? Where are the original text books *(for school, college and university)* written on technical, medical and scientific subjects and particularly the research journals in these languages? Where are the scientists who are technically qualified to read, write, comprehend and think and create new knowledge in local regional languages? And above all, where are efficient scientific and technical translators and translation bureaus for the purposes? I do not wish to propose that nothing has been done at all in this area but what ever has been done so, is too meager and often haphazard for an impact even at the individual State levels. Almost all national languages are being gradually marginalized for only restricted use in local literature, communication, films, theatre plays, entertainment and such other use rather than into a proficient, vibrant, active mode of communication for technical, scientific and medical education, research, administration and developmental purposes. The reason being; a clear discrimination against educated youth through regional languages in preference for those from the English medium for job opportunities under Central Government which carry better scales of pay than offered by the State Governments. The Central Government on its part has also failed to fulfill its constitutional obligation of switching over to Hindi for official work. I am certainly not against learning English or any other foreign language but at the same time, I am confident that every language of the country is equally strong and easy for abstract scientific communication. Only a beginning has to be made in exclusively communicating science and research in these languages on the part of scientists and technologists themselves. In fact, any proficient multi lingual individual enjoys greater social preference and acceptability within linguistic communities. The three language formula of compulsory teaching of Hindi, English and the regional state language within schools was the best bet for the country but the seriousness, emphasis and even encouragement for acquiring and ensuring proficiency *(in reading, writing and speaking)* in three languages is surely lacking on the part of the linguistic state governments and even as a realization for enlightened citizenship by individuals. Unless the original thoughts do not arise in our minds in the language we use, so long as we fall short of proficiency. And without command over language, there is always a chance to fall as a victim for misunderstanding, word twisting, reason and logic.

11

The Need for Reorientation of Policies on Science Education: My Perceptions

A conscious national policy after the independence in 1947 should have been to provide a vigorous support to put our traditional science, wisdom, use of specific ingredients in specific medicinal practices, and knowledge supported with modern experimental evidence and scientific terminology. In a way all that we traditionally believed and practically followed should have been revalidated on the basis of modern scientific theories, concepts, principles, instrumental techniques and practically documented results based on statistical tests of significance, rather than leaving everything on emotional appeal or even emotional blackmail of a vast majority of illiterate or semi-literate population. Based on this strategy, proven results and patented applications, even the Western scientifically advanced countries would have willingly accepted our traditional science as something of continued alternate value and use. To a great extent, this has been gradually successful in respect of at least our traditional Science of Yoga, Meditation and Mind and thought control in relation of human physiology, relaxation and good health. Similar approach is needed in respect of several other areas and more particularly– Ayurveda and Ayurvedic medicines and practices. Such an approach has been exemplified recently by Professor S. Chandrasekhar, Nobel Laureate, in re-writing the celebrated book by Sir Isaac Newton- *'Philosophiæ Naturalis Principia Mathematica, in Latin* for 'Mathematical Principles of Natural Philosophy', often called the '*Principia'* ('Principles') published in July 1687 into modern mathematical notations, ***(Reference 15).*** A similar lead with a fervent urge, as I believe, has to be provided by the scientists from within the country. I wish our scientists; policy makers and science administrators concentrate more on our national priorities and problems for solutions than to waste time, resources and manpower on problems and priorities of the western countries, having only hypothetical or very little relevance to our situations. This kind of national policy would be helpful in not only putting our ancient science on modern scientific basis but would generate employment to millions in rural and forest areas in conservation, cultivation, preservation, processing and even marketing of our medicinal herbs, plants, trees, fruits from various locations besides protecting theft of our biodiversity.

Brighter and enthusiast amongst the science educated youth could have been put on jobs of instrument based characterization of our medicinal and herb-plants in all respects including identification of the molecules of medicinal or commercial importance as their constituents, their isolation, purification, concentration and efficacy in remedial treatments, filing patents and formulating commercial products. This is all the more urgent because nearly ninety percent of our ancient literature on Ayurveda has already been destroyed by the barbarian Muslim invaders who came here from across the western borders of India in search of treasures to loot. It has been well documented that in the absence of any fire-fighting equipments and such means, the library of the Nalanda University in present Bihar, which was set on fire by the invading army under Bakhtiyar Khilji in 1193 AD, was burning for over three months. This can give us the idea of the number of books, ancient records on tree leaves, metal plates etc that must have been destroyed in this fire. Only illiterate, un-thoughtful and un-civilized individuals could have indulged into such vandalizing acts.

12

What is Needed is a Change of Mindset

The whole exercise needs a complete change in mindset and orientation in our adoption of an educational system. In this context, I would also like our scientists to publish their first rate research papers in our own journals than to send them to journals published in other countries to enhance value and circulation of their periodicals. It is unfortunate that many of our indigenous research journals of registered professional scientific societies are lagging behind in national and international circulation, regularity in publication, efficient and intellectually honest referral and review system, quality of research papers recommended and published and quality of printing besides ethical and professional management of the whole gamete of scientific publication. Is this not a matter of concern that despite having more than 45 Agricultural Universities and a huge empire of exclusive Directorates on specific crops, Central Institutes, National Research Centres, Krishi Vigyan Kendras and various other organizations under the Indian Council of Agricultural Research (ICAR), over 500 universities under the University Grants Commission (UGC), and an equal number of other research laboratories under various ministries and organizations, our research journals in general, should be suffering from poor subscriptions *(both individual and institutional)*, circulation, readership, quality of contributed articles, production and of course in the international impact factors? Many of these journals are not being lifted in full by the national and international abstracting journals even decades after being in regular publication since inception. Further, scientists must be encouraged to subscribe at least four professional journals and buy two books annually in his / her area of specialization and be allowed income tax relief for upkeep of his professional requirement. If savings in provident fund or some economic growth and management related schemes of the government qualify for tax benefits and rebates, subscriptions for professional journals must also be allowed, as an incentive measure in the larger interest of the society and the nation at large, as a part of the conscious long-term scientific research and development policy. After all, nation will only look to the locally available professional scientists and qualified human resource in case of emergent need and it is the moral duty of the sovereign government to help the professional scientists in keeping themselves up to date in their skills through such small measures. A nation is after all known and recognized more from the quality of its socially progressive and sagacious leadership, professionally competent scientific, technological, medical and military manpower and level of literacy than from any other stray economic considerations of GNP or GDP, Balance of Trade or rise and fall of stock market index etc. despite considerably unjustified and disproportionate economic importance attached to them.

We are living in an age in which economics depends on technology and technology in turn depends on science, very largely on physics. Economics therefore follows a strong scientific and technological society ahead rather than the other way round. A globally competitive technical, scientific and medical human resource is always an asset to a nation and rulers *(from all shades of political philosophies)* must understand to value, respect and support it by all possible means and at whatever price. It is these kinds of professionals who not only build nations and sustain pressure on local administrative machinery for developing infrastructure and its maintenance but act as catalysts for a positive change to create wealth. The secret of affluent nations today is that their political leadership is aware of the fact that only science and technology can take nations to greater heights and only spread of scientific awareness and education amongst people can bring harmony, progress and prosperity. No wonder, America beckons and imports the best of talents from all over the world irrespective of caste, creed, religion or nationality, just provides them with challenges, encouragement, financial support, opportunities and freedom to prove and reap the benefits of their labour in developing technologies for the future. Unless there is a collective drastic change in the mindset of our politicians and leaders in India, progress will remain dismally slow. The young and youthful Prime Minister of India Late Mr. Rajeev Gandhi, perhaps, frustrated with the kind of mindset of our elected politicians around, had once remarked during parliamentary debate on 'Brain Drain from India' that- "It is better to allow brain drain than to keep our brains in the drains here".

13

Agricultural Physics in India

In one of the most foresighted decisions, taken within the first decade of the shifting of the then 'Imperial Agricultural Research Institute' to Delhi in 1936 from a village called Pusa in the state of Bihar, a small nucleus cell- 'Physics in agriculture' was created in 1948. Dr. C. Dakshinamurti **(Fig.1)** who had returned from Rothamstad Experimental Station, after completing his Doctorate from the University of London, was appointed as Experimental Physicist, a post created within the erstwhile Division of Agricultural Chemistry of the institute. Dr. J. N. Mukherjee, the then Director-IARI and Prof. K. S. Krishnan, Founder Director of the National Physical Laboratory had played a very crucial role in the introduction and teaching of physics at the institute. With support and blessing from Dr. Homi Jehangir (H. J.) Bhabha, the architect of Indian atomic research and nuclear energy programmes, the nucleus cell 'Physics in Agriculture' at the IARI was expanded into a 'Unit of Physics' in 1955, and then into a permanent research and teaching division of 'Agricultural Physics' in 1962, after the institute was granted the status of a Deemed University in 1958. Ever since then, research, teaching and programmes of the division have given new directions and dimensions to the conduct of research in a holistic way. Soil Physics, Biophysics, Meteorology and Remote Sensing (as modified from spectroscopy) have been the sub divisions of the discipline of Agricultural Physics and students are imparted courses in all these areas of sub divisions. With blessings, encouragement and support from none other than Dr. C. Dakshinamurti, it was my privilege and honour to compile and publish a comprehensive document on the history and contributions in Agricultural Physics in India *('Four Decades of Research in Agricultural Physics (1962-2002)' Published by the Division of Agricultural Physics, Indian Agricultural Research Institute, New Delhi, India, 2003, Editor A.V. Moharir, et. al.* ***(Reference.16)*** during my headship of the Division and also to convene a National Symposium on the occasion of completing four decades of the establishment of the discipline of Agricultural Physics. On this occasion, I designed a special emblem for the Division of Agricultural Physics **(Fig.9)** consisting of an outer Solar Rim, the source of energy on the earth, enclosing the Yin and Yang symbol symbolizing the law of complementarity at the base of all creation in nature with Einstein's equation of energy–mass equivalence, representing the only fundamental truth of nature in its manifestation, superimposed over it. The words –"Physics in Agriculture: Complementarity in Nature" were put under the emblem, justifying the philosophy that laws of physics form the undercurrent behind all material or biological creation and activities in nature. This emblem was adopted and printed on the book referred above ***(Reference.16, Fig. 9).***

FOUR DECADES OF RESEARCH
IN
AGRICULTURAL PHYSICS

(1962-2002)

PHYSICS IN AGRICULTURE

COMPLEMENTARITY IN NATURE

Division of Agricultural Physics
Indian Agricultural Research Institute
New Delhi-110 012

April, 2003

DIVISION OF AGRICULTURAL PHYSICS

(Established 1962)

PHYSICS IN AGRICULTURE

COMPLEMENTARITY IN NATURE

INDIAN AGRICULTURAL RESEARCH INSTITUTE,
PUSA CAMPUS, NEW DELHI-110012, INDIA

Telephone : +91-11-2578 1178, +91-11-2578 8853
Telefax : +91-11-2586 2321, Telex : 3177161-IARI IN
Telegram : Agriphysics-KRISHIPUSA, New Delhi-110012
Website: www.iaripusa.org

Figure 9: a. Four Decades of Research in Agricultural Physics, Facsmile of Book; b. First information brochure with emblem designed for the Division of Agricultural Physics

The first ever printed information folder describing history, objectives, mission, achievements, present projects in hand and future perspectives of the Division was also brought out later during my headship. By the year 2003, more than two hundred students had received their M.Sc. and Ph.D. degrees from the discipline of Agricultural Physics.

14

Indian Agricultural Research Institute (IARI) and its Post Graduate School System

Commercial cultivation of crop plants is essentially a multidisciplinary endeavor for maximizing yield. The fundamental principles of scientific crop cultivation of various crop types have been elaborated extensively in our Vedic literature. They withstand the most rigorous modern scientific reasoning and logic even today. Unfortunately, continued, intentional neglect of mass education and literacy over several centuries during barbarous Mughal and later British control of political governance of India, known to history, eroded the basic aptitude of our people and farmers in particular to look to cultivation of crops on scientific basis. And the farming, gradually changed into more as a traditional family endeavour devoid of innovations, scientific and technical inputs and genetic improvement of crop species to suit new demands on yields and quality. In the process, the best of brains from among the farmer families from all states of the country got diverted to other lucrative areas such as literature, engineering, architecture, medicine, armed forces, commercial trade and such other professions. In the absence of mechanized power tools, implements, quality seeds, irrigation facilities, conservation of perennial water bodies, new knowledge on agronomic practices and mental preparedness for rigorous physical exertion required in farming profession, further alienated those with poor physical fitness from agriculture. Therefore, when some judicious British Government officials decided to put Indian Agriculture on modern scientific foundation and established Agricultural Research Institutes at various places across the country in 1905, scientists from the so called pure disciplines were recruited and transformed into 'professional 'agricultural scientists' for conducting research on problems related to the commercial cultivation of agricultural crops and their improvement in terms of quality and yields. There was no discrimination of any kind between various scientific disciplines in recruiting and constituting research teams/ units. The scientists on their part, irrespective of their training and specialization at the master's or doctoral degree level, were also flexible in attitude, eager to learn, accept new challenges, diversify their knowledge, develop new expertise and practically contribute to problems outside their own specialty areas with sincerity of purpose. No wonder, all the celebrated names associated with transforming the global and post-independence agriculture in India, were all converts from pure scientific disciplines. Dr. Norman E. Borlaug (Nobel Laureate) the breeder of high yielding, fertilizer responsive, Mexican dwarf wheat varieties was a originally a man of forestry who turned to genetics and plant breeding and Dr. B. P. Pal, Dr. A. B. Joshi, Dr. M. S. Swaminathan, Dr. R. J. Kalamkar, Dr. M. V. Rao, Dr. H. K. Jain, Dr. B. R. Murty, Dr. M. N. Paithankar, Dr. M. W. Hardas, Dr. V. L. Chopra and several others were pure botanists by training. It was not uncommon to find a pure physicist heading the division of soil science or a plant physiologist heading the division of Agronomy. Even, all agricultural research and teaching activities were conducted under the Divisions / Departments named after pure scientific disciplines, such as Division of botany, chemistry, physics, mathematics and statistics etc. However, the scenario changed drastically after the establishment of exclusive 'Agricultural Universities following the recommendations of the Professor Daulat Singh (D. S.) Kothari Commission on Education and integration of all agriculture related teaching, research, education, training, extension and policy formulation activities as a national endeavor, under the enlarged and re-organized Indian Council of Agricultural Research in 1965.

The Imperial Agricultural Research Institute, originally established in 1905 at Pusa Bihar, was re-located in the foothills of the last traces of the Aravali mountain ranges in New Delhi in 1936, after its magnificent building called 'Navlakha' at Pusa-Bihar, was destroyed in a massive earthquake. After independence, its name was changed to Indian Agricultural Research Institute and it got recognized popularly as 'Pusa Institute' for reasons of its earlier location. Today, even the name 'Pusa' as an appendage to all the crop, vegetable and flower varieties, released from the institute (IARI), stands patented for intellectual property rights. The institute saw various changes during its existence in Delhi and its administration and management was finally transferred to the Indian Council of Agricultural Research with deemed to be university status under the UGC act in 1958. The Post Graduate School was formally established and the institute started imparting teaching and training and award of its own M.Sc. and Ph.D. degrees. Its earlier Diploma in Associate ship of IARI was recognized as equivalent to M.Sc. degree [1-3].

15

The First Regular Dean of PG-School

The institute was lucky in getting from amongst its employees, one of the best, innovative, progressive, cultured scientist and eloquent teacher in Dr. Atmaram Bhairav (A. B.) Joshi as the first regular Dean of its Post Graduate School. Dr. A. B. Joshi, not only laid the foundation of the school but he turned it into one of the foremost educational institution in Agriculture. This was evident later from the kind of role the institute played in ushering the first ever, 'proverbial green revolution' in the country and saved millions of people from the sub-continent from starvation. Today, India holds unprecedented buffer stocks of food grains in its silos[4].

As the first Dean, Dr. A. B. Joshi organized the entire functioning of the Post Graduate School, modified and framed new rules and regulations, strengthened multi-disciplinary research with such mandatory constitution of students advisory committees in every discipline and set rigorous procedures for evaluation of thesis. He introduced the innovative concept of various schools of 'Crop Production', 'Crop Protection', 'Basic Sciences', 'Natural Resource Management' and 'Extension Education' to define areas of overall teaching and research activities of the institute. As a logical fall out, he was also instrumental in the constitution of separate Academic, Research and Extension Councils for the working of the re-organized institute. The positions of Dean and Joint Director (Education); Joint Director (Research); Joint Director (Extension) and Joint Director (Administration) owe their origin to Dr. A. B. Joshi to a great extent. The constitution of various 'Standing Committees' under the chairmanship of renowned and sagacious Professors for proposing new changes, resolving controversies, interpretation of rules, courses and curriculum, faculty induction, staff and students grievances and such other matters, added further dimensions to the smooth functioning of the Post-Graduate School in IARI. These Standing Committees have served exceedingly well in their advisory roles to the Institute Academic Council [2]. However, as a faculty member for over three decades in IARI, it was my observation that not many students were aware and conversant about the factual role of inter-play of energy and matter in our daily life and for that matter in our very existence. With considerable efforts and persuasions in the standing committee meetings on courses and curriculum, a course on 'Energy Basis of Nature' was introduced at my initiative in the Division of Agricultural Physics with the hope that this would be a mandatory core course for not only the students of the Agricultural Physics division but from other disciplines as well. After all, every activity in agriculture be it pathology, genetics or agronomy are nothing more than an inter-play of only matter and energy and it was my conviction that every student must be fully aware of this. Unfortunately, the chairmen of student's thesis advisory committees on pretext of time-bound submission of thesis, completion of mandatory course credits and lack of time, did not find it necessary, even on academic merit to prepare their students in understanding the fundamentals of energy basis of universal existence. Instead, there was an intense feeling that mandatory courses on 'History and Philosophy of Science or Philosophy of life or Biology' may go a long way in developing scientific temper, admiration for scientists and their work, developing passion to contribute and in evolving a positive scientific culture.

16

The PG-School System of IARI

The Post Graduate School System of the Indian Agricultural Research Institute, its procedures, rules and administration is perhaps the best in the country. No surprise the IARI has maintained its position as a foremost institute in the country for research in agriculture. This system has withstood the test of times for over sixty four years ever since its inception and implementation in 1958. Since then, very few major modifications in basic structural framework of administration have been made except in case of the revisions, new introductions and deletions of several courses and their contents, and inclusion of some new research and teaching disciplines such as Agricultural Physics, Agricultural Chemicals, Plant Physiology, Molecular Biology and Biotechnology, Water Science and Technology, Post-Harvest Technology, Plant Genetic Resource and Floriculture, as was demanded from time to time. By and large, many of the procedures adopted, traditions invoked, rituals established and observed in the conduct of Post Graduate School activities, practically continue to be as they were laid at the time of the establishment of the Post Graduate School. This is a proof of the foresighted wisdom of Dr. A. B. Joshi and his celebrated colleagues, who framed the basic and operational structure for the working of the P.G. School. However, it was due entirely to the credit of Dr. Kissen Kanungo, Dean and Joint Director (Education) in succession, who compiled, edited and printed all the rules, regulations, procedural forms, formats of several examinations and evaluation proforma and list of courses along with discipline wise syllabus, names of course leaders, faculty members etc in the form of a book popularly called the 'Green Book' of the PG School calendar.

17

Contribution to Strengthening Language Proficiency

Post Graduate School used to have a regular post of Assistant Professor of English to teach English language and help students in editing their thesis and research papers, considering the poor background of language among students belonging to the rural areas. Regretfully, this post of assistant professor of English has been discontinued for reasons not known, after the last incumbent retired from service. Even foreign languages such as German and Russian were also being taught by some of the proficient institute faculty in evening classes and these classes used to be very popular. Learning languages should always be encouraged and knowing several languages is always an asset for any civilized individual.

How I wish, IARI should also test students for written and oral proficiency in English as an essential part of its entrance examination. Students, admitted without fluency in the language of instruction and communication become liabilities on their chairmen guiding their M.Sc. or Ph. D. thesis. And I am of my considered opinion that unless the institute authorities consciously set proficiency in language of instruction as a precondition for admission, students will not convert that into an inner urge to improve and even excel.

18

Entrance Examination for Admission to IARI: Merit and Demerits

The introduction of All India Competitive Entrance Examination, exclusively for Admission to M.Sc. and Ph.D. courses in IARI has undoubtedly enlarged the base and elevated the standard and quality of admitted students in some disciplines. However, the desired results have not changed very significantly in case of some other disciplines like Agricultural Physics, Biochemistry, Nematology, Water Science and Technology, Plant Genetic Resources etc. Gradually, the level of mediocrity is growing fast and is alarming within these disciplines. The reasons for this may perhaps be lying somewhere else rather than in the conduct of the entrance tests but more plausibly in the pattern of the mandatory examination paper on agriculture, which in my personal opinion acts more as a filter to reject the students from the pure disciplines than serving any useful purpose. I feel strongly to let talent from everywhere get into the system on academic merit and then mould them for your specific needs and priorities. As an, example, I am personally at pains to observe, why not a single student with pure M.Sc. Physics background should not have qualified and admitted to the discipline of Agricultural Physics through the competitive entrance examination for Ph.D. degree in the last four decades? This has not only defeated the purpose of establishing the discipline to some extent but has resulted into a dominant shift to study of problems more in relation to soil, meteorology and agronomic practices in preference to application or elucidation of physical principles involved in all aspects of plant growth and their yields. Situation in other hybrid disciplines is no better either and certainly calls for thorough review. This also puts the faculty to a great disadvantage in assigning challenging research problems to students getting admitted to these disciplines from agriculture background without a strong basic knowledge of physics, chemistry and mathematics. Agricultural Physics has turned itself over the years into a fertile ground for inbreeding with serious handicap for developing innovative multi-disciplinary research teams, known nationally and internationally for innovative programs in plant biophysics, molecular biophysics and ultra-structure, use and application of nuclear and other sophisticated physical instrumental techniques and instrumentation. It is more intriguing and surprising for me, that despite some very exemplary contributions of the Division of Agricultural Physics from IARI since 1962, and continued relevance and importance in understanding the basic science behind all processes in agricultural production, why the Indian Council of Agricultural Research (ICAR) should not have been encouraged to establish this discipline in some other central and state agricultural universities? And today, there are more than one hundred odd agricultural universities in the country. On the contrary, and more surprisingly, a very disastrous and foolish decision was taken some years ago by the Agricultural Scientists Recruitment Board (ASRB) in that they removed the subject of Physics from their list for recruitment of scientists through Agricultural Research Service (ARS) Examination.

The philosophy of selection through competitive entrance examination should be to encourage the best among all the pure and applied disciplines to accept challenging opportunities of working in multidisciplinary areas of agricultural research and education. It should be broad based and not restrictive, both from the point of view of related disciplines and number of students competing. It should certainly not be allowed to become a green pasture, restricted to students passing out of the moulds of some narrow disciplines from within the institute and other agricultural universities, as is certainly the case today. This statement has two aspects; (1)- a false sense of view that IARIs' own students are better and they fare well and (2)- there is still much to be desired from those passing out of other state agricultural universities, which have become, victims of inbreeding, lack of competitive spirit and reserved pastures for the students of mushrooming agricultural colleges and universities. I would personally prefer an open selection based on rigorous personal interviews besides a short written test in subject specialty area for knowledge, history and philosophy of science and more for scientific aptitude, sincerity, integrity and convictions. There are many proven psycho-analytical methods now available to scientifically assess these apparently subjective qualities. And full use should be made of them in improving the quality of human resource required for a scientific research career. However, the most important advantage of the introduction of the Entrance Examination for admission in IARI being, that it has been able to ward off unsolicited recommendations, undue pressures, political or other influences, personal or regional bias and back-door entries. What is then required is to improve it still further in terms of the nature, pattern, quality and type of questions framed for examination.

19

Misuse of Infrastructure Facilities by Students with No Convictions

A deplorable consequence of admitting students with deceptive intentions, divided convictions and insincerity of purpose can be witnessed from the ever increasing number of IARI students competing in the state and central civil service examinations (UPSC) annually while staying and enjoying IARI hostel and other facilities and comfortable monetary support in terms of student fellowship and research grant. It is no secret that students competing for the civil services examinations *(without official permission)* are highly irregular, negligent and even indulging into malpractice of marking attendance by proxy for the period during their preparation and examination dates. As students of science, craving for a career in scientific research through a successful entry in IARI through entrance examination, such seemingly innocent or justifiable actions for whatever reasons should not be tolerated. Personally, I consider these students to be cheating and diluting the purpose, efforts and resources of the institute for improving its own research efforts and academic standard.

I also personally feel that the institute should take no pride in case of students getting selected for such civil services. There is no credit but only discredit to the institute because, the institute has no mandate and does not prepare students for civil services. Moreover, it is a reflection on the procedures being followed for admission of students for Ph.D. and M.Sc. programs in that, the institute is admitting even those who are not serious about taking scientific agricultural research as a career with sincere convictions or consider it as a second or last option despite securing entry through written examination. I am afraid, if IARI-admission entrance examination over the years has become pliable to strategic planning for cracking than a test of scientific aptitude and caliber? Perhaps a pattern adopted by the Indian Institutes of Technology (IIT's) for their common admission test may prove better.

What is true about student's admission procedure is also true about the recruitment of scientists through a written and oral examination of the Agricultural Scientists Recruitment

Board. If passing examinations were to be a reliable measure of scientific caliber, aptitude or abilities, ICAR should have witnessed by now a vigorous, ebullient scientific temper and productivity of creative output among its scientist cadre after more than sixty years of running the recruitment policy through the ARS examination system. A rough indication of this malaise can be seen from the fact that no 'Shanti Swaroop Bhatnagar Award', the highest recognition for scientific research in India, has come to any IARI scientist ever since 1986. Professor S. K. Sinha, former Director-IARI and National Professor of Eminence, could envisage and foresee the ailing symptoms of such Agricultural Research Service Recruitment System and therefore he had emphatically pleaded for closing it down in his 29 th Lal Bahadur Shastri Memorial Lecture delivered at IARI on April 14,1999. It is no secret that many among the presently employed exist here just because there is employment. After all, conducting good teaching, training and innovative research is the first and foremost priority of IARI and cannot be left to suffer on account of mediocrity. Unless each and every member of a 'research-team' is not inflamed with the same passion and conviction to crack a particular research problem, no worthwhile research can be anticipated. History of modern science is a record of such intense passions, convictions and sincerity of purpose upheld by the pioneers behind their success. A true student of science or a scientist must understand his / her own discipline; know its foundation and roots of their connectivity to the apparent problem in hand rather than turning himself into a technically sophisticated but intellectually sterile drone.

20

Provision of Remedial Course Work for Non-Agriculture Students and Multi-Disciplinary Research

IARI has an excellent provision of prescribing 'Remedial Course work' for students, occasionally admitted from non-agriculture background or deputed from a foreign country under some exchange program of the government of India with various countries. If this is indeed so, there appears little relevance or justification of subjecting them to a mandatory question paper on agriculture at the time of the competitive entrance test for admission to M.Sc. and Ph.D. degrees. Even if this is felt absolutely necessary, the questions framed under this paper should purely be of a level, answers to which are expected of any civilized and reasonably well educated student of science. This distinction is very thin and it is here, most students from the pure disciplines had been falling victim to the incorrectly chosen or framed questions. All questions should be carefully discriminated and selected. Instead, I would prefer a mandatory question paper on the history of agriculture and philosophy of science together with psychoanalyses of candidates to assess scientific and intellectual integrity, aptitude and convictions for a scientific research career.

It would be interesting to recall here, my free and frank discussion on this subject with Dr. A. B. Joshi, knowing well that he was the architect of the creation of exclusive Agricultural University system in the country as a member of the Professor D. S. Kothari Commission on Education Reforms. I told him very frankly that I was observing a gradual decline in appreciation of the importance of fundamental basic disciplines such as botany, chemistry and physics in the institute (IARI). There were distinct tendencies among agricultural scientists to keep persons from so-called pure disciplines at a distance and from involvement in pursuit of research objectives. I also told him, that if such trend continues for another two or three decades, perhaps it would be realized later, that creation of exclusive agricultural universities was a mistake, and it may then be too late for any corrective measures. He paused for a moment and then said with a long breath- "I consider myself to be first a Botanist and then an Agricultural Scientist. The Change from botany to agricultural research was a big challenge for me, but even so, I enjoyed very much and felt quite happy. As a Botanist, I now gained knowledge about agricultural science and development in the 'economic sense'. Dr. Joshi did not like compartmentalization in scientific disciplines and had gone on record to say- "If in any research institute, inter-disciplinary, inter-personal, goal-oriented scientific discussion does not take place, such an institute, no matter whether big or small, can be pronounced as dead".

In this context, I would like to take example of our own 'Indian Institute of Technology' established initially at five places in the country with technical and scientific assistance from USA, Britain and Russia (USSR). All these are exclusively technology and engineering-oriented institutes and yet, they support, encourage and maintain very strong independent departments of Physics, Mathematics, Chemistry, Biotechnology, social sciences and several other interdisciplinary schools under nationally or internationally established scientists. There is a great lesson for those concerned with research, education, training, extension and technologies of agricultural production. Any neglect of teaching basic disciplines and strong practical support in our exclusive agricultural universities will lead to their slow poisoning and ultimately death.

There is also something of concern about the evaluation of M.Sc. and Ph.D. thesis in recent times. Whereas, I can understand a time-bound submission, evaluation and award of degree in case of M.Sc. student, such haste in clearing a Ph.D. thesis before the convocation deadline is unwarranted. The author witnessed award of doctorate degree to students on very cursory, casual, one or one and a half page reports from examiners and without rigorously critical, scholarly, scientific and competent evaluation of the thesis-research problem. Should only the signed statement by the examiner-'I recommend the student for the award of the degree of Master of Science or Doctor of Philosophy' at the end of his 'casual report' be considered sufficient for awarding a degree to the student? Similarly, if thorough evaluation of every research thesis by a competent subject specialist is the primary objective, there is no justification for the PG school administration to always find the nearest examiner (around New Delhi or from among the ICAR System only) for evaluation. I would personally like the IARI-thesis being evaluated by well-known specialists irrespective of they being Indian or foreigners. After all we do subject our piece of good research to subject-specialist reviewers when we communicate it to an international journal for acceptance, priority and publication. The evaluation of research-thesis should also be done in the same spirit in the interest of science, which I consider to be the only 'Universal Religion' of mankind. Ideally, the Ph.D. thesis in IARI should be a total fulfillment of the requirement and not a partial fulfillment as it is today. The choice of course work for Ph.D. student should be limited to supplement his knowledge for gaps in relation to his personal training and proposed research problem.

21

Dual Faculty Membership in Post Graduate School

As discussed earlier, agriculture being essentially a multidisciplinary, multi-specialty enterprise for maximization of crop yields, it is expected that the most successful persons are those who by their own conscious efforts evolved themselves into rare hybrids between disciplines. And there are several individuals who had demonstrated themselves of possessing such capacity with their creative contribution. Therefore, IARI became the first institute to not only recognize this fact to encourage building up of such rare human resource but tried to introduce dual faculty membership in such exceptional cases. A positive decision in favour of granting dual faculty membership would have enlarged the perspective of students working under such faculty and encouraged them to cross boundaries of disciplines to their own advantage. Dual faculty membership was not conceived as a general rule applicable to every faculty member but as an honor for those who deserved. Such a multi-disciplinary faculty member can easily meet any shortfall arising in any other related disciplines when demanded.

22

Emerging Challenges to Universities in General

The most serious challenges that have emerged in the last few years to all the conventional and agricultural universities and other educational institutions in the country without exception of IARI, being;

1. Drastic fall in the number of students interested in studying pure and applied sciences.
2. Increase in number of students dropping out in the middle of the courses in preference to other services.
3. Increasing preference among students for Administrative, Banking and Management streams in view of lucrative glitter *(a mirage)* of working conditions, salaries in the management / business related jobs.
4. Lack of responsive, efficient and transparent institutional mechanism for early appreciation and recognition for good scientific work.
5. Out-dated, incompatible bureaucratic administrative and audit system enforced in scientific and research institutions.
6. Tedious, long drawn wasteful procedures, *often sabotaged by vested interests,* adopted for purchase of stores for timely conduct of experiments in laboratories and procedures for disposal of the unserviceable stores and equipment.
7. Practical absence of a conscious policy on the part of the institute for automatic regular up-gradation of capital-intensive existing instrumental facilities, and scientifically trained technical manpower for their maintenance and use in research programs.
8. Likewise, there is need for introducing computerized administration in the Post Graduate School so that both the faculty and students remain in constant touch with each other.
9. The Library of IARI, which is a *de facto* National Library on Agriculture, needs to be nurtured with utmost care, adequate funds and their timely release for utilization. There is gradual decline of the number of journals from the subscription list, and even the established journals with a continuity of several decades being subscribed ever

since the establishment of the institute and more are under threat of discontinuation for want of adequate funds. There is a pressure and fancy for subscribing more of digital online versions of these journals for the library. However, online journals have their own problems, limitations and utility value for commercial reasons. The perpetual problem of uncertainty of the quantum and time of release of funds has put the library staff to great harassment and disillusion in view of the rising subscription cost of journals and periodicals. At the same time, there is also an increasing and justified demand to subscribe new journals emerging in very narrow specialized areas without corresponding increase in the allotted budget.

10. Little or practically no encouragement for personal initiative suppresses creativity, promoting a general apathy and lethargy among the young minds for any radical change. They should not be encouraged to only receive commands and obey. This is unscientific and detrimental to building a healthy scientific environment, temper, culture of free and frank discussion, tradition and the Institution in general. However, personal initiative does not mean total liberty but a definite discipline of mind, mutual respect, intention, conduct, open discussion, consensus and then collective execution.
11. Youth in the country (with exceptions) are seeking white collar jobs in preference over creative, challenging and entrepreneurial efforts; on the strength of their learning and seem to be least prepared for some personal sacrifice.
12. Agricultural produce, food and horticultural processing in India have a tremendous potential and scope for a motivated individual. And it is here, the Agricultural University education needs to be predominantly oriented in training two streams of individuals; one for practical skills in processing, managing and running the enterprise and second in conducting basic research on all aspects of production, processing, preservation, packaging, material characterization, quality control, transportation, storage and marketing of various processed food and horticultural products. This leaves tremendous unlimited scope for research and developmental activities with specifics to individual crop / fruit / spice / herbs etc. and generate entrepreneurial and employment opportunities. The research-oriented jobs, of course can be left for the benefit of those who are good in fundamental science, are creative, innovative and original thinking besides being serious in taking up a research career with sincerity and convictions.
13. It is in this context, there is urgent need to open the doors of agricultural universities for a free flow of students and faculty from both basic and applied disciplines to take up research in areas of agriculture. Agriculture by its very composition is essentially a multi-disciplinary multi-trade enterprise. The current practice of restricting admission in most of our agricultural universities to only graduates and postgraduates from agricultural sciences would be suicidal in the long run. The

Agricultural universities have much to learn from the composition, frameworks and structures of our Indian Institutes of Technologies.

14. Fortunately, the demand and employment record of IARI students from all the disciplines so far is generally good but the institute cannot be complacent and need to be vigilant to the trend and requirement of the prospective job market in the light of the fact that agriculture is evolving into globally competitive and knowledge intensive vocation.

Life of an individual, institution or a nation is always cyclic with periodic phases of difficulties, glory and defeat. Our persistent endeavor should be to reduce the damaging intensity and amplitude of these cyclic phases to as minimum as possible for continued success. In this respect, the National Disaster Management Teams / Schemes launched and organized by the Government of India at the national and state levels is a very thoughtful decision. What matters in the life of an institution is a chain of dedicated leadership at the helm and committed band of scientific workers to carry forward the tradition of doing good science. Success lies in the selection and recruitment of competent and eager scientific personnel, providing congenial environment, opportunities, encouragement and recognition *(without asking or seeking)* to the rightful individuals. A Sovereign Independent Nation can only survive and progress on the strength of its own technological development and quality of its own technical and scientific human resource. Progress can never be sustained on borrowed technologies for long. I have no doubt that despite some odds and aberrations at times, IARI with its wonderful Post Graduate School System, backed up by infrastructure facilities will ever remain reverberating into its glorious phase because it has been built on a very sound academic and administrative structure of its post graduate school. I only wish, the ICAR authorities do not indulge in fragmentation of this great institute and keep on creating institutes within institute on its land.

For further reading

1. 'Naulakha (Tale of a forgotten township)', Bishad K. Mukherjee, 1992, Published by the author, New Delhi.
2. 'Indian Agricultural Research Institute, Golden Jubilee Publication', IARI, 1955, New Delhi, 110012.
3. 'Souvenir, Golden Jubilee, 1905-1955', Indian Agricultural Research Institute, 1955, New Delhi, 10012.
4. 'Profile in Solitude-Felicitation of Professor A.B. Joshi on his Ninety First birthday', A.V. Moharir, Editor, November 2007. Private Publication by Mrs. Vimala A. Joshi, A-408, Vasundhara Apartments, Sector-6, Plot-16, Dwarka, New Delhi, 110075.

23

Initiation into Professional Agricultural Physics

Working with Dr. G. S. R. Krishnamurti, I was given the work of estimating the iron content in aqueous extracts of soils after oxidation of organic matter with hydrogen peroxide. In the process, I realized that the spectrophotometer procedure (due to M. L. Jackson et. al.) that I was given to me to use was not repetitively accurate and giving full recovery of iron. This led me to improvise and develop my own new procedure using thioglycolic acid to reduce ferric iron into ferrous form and then use 1,10- orthophenanthroline to produce a stable orange coloured complex with a linear relation between iron content and spectral absorbance, over a large range of concentration. The new method involved no heating of sample aliquots for full colour development *(as was required in Jackson's method)*, but only addition of reagents at room temperature and read absorbance on a spectrophotometer. The colour developed was absolutely stable for over six months and recovery of iron was hundred percent. Besides, the method showed no interference from a large number of chemical ions commonly found in soils, in very large concentrations. This made the procedure especially advantageous, quick and reliable when determinations on a large number of soil samples were involved, moreover the stability of the ferrous-orthophenanthroline coloured complex for over six months enabled sufficient leisure for measurement of absorbance. This success in developing a new method for trace determination of iron and particularly the use of thioglycolic acid for reducing ferric iron encouraged me to try this in suppressing interference of ferric ions in the trace determination of Titanium with TIRON (disodium 1, 2-dihydroxybenzene 3-5 disulfonate). Here, I observed that one milliliter of 40% thioglycolic acid did the trick in completely preventing interference from ferric ions in developing Titanium-TIRON coloured complex with full recovery of titanium and also without interference from several other chemical ions in high concentrations commonly found in soils. The two new methods for determination of iron and titanium came out to be my first research papers in print in an international journal within two and half years of my taking a plunge in the area of Agricultural Physics and were a real pleasure to me and my mother who had taken all pains since my childhood for my education and upbringing.

There were no computers, e-libraries, PDF files and internet connections and even Xerox photo copiers in those times in India. All requests for copies of research papers were sent and received through reprint request cards. And within three months of publishing my first research papers, requests for copies of the reprints were virtually raining on my desk from all scientifically progressive countries and from all continents. The authors in those days, used to receive only 25 copies of the reprints gratis from the publishers and those were certainly not enough to satisfy and honour the requests from distant scientists. In view of scarce foreign exchange position of the country in those years, there was taboo on purchase of additional reprints as a matter of institute policy. I had no option but to go in for photographic reproductions of these two papers and satisfy the demand for copies at my personal cost for both photo copies and international postage. The Divisional administration was reluctant to spend money on international postage in response to requests in such large number because international postage was also prohibitively expensive in those days in India. I preserved most of these early reprint request cards as mementoes until recently, which gave me a satisfying pleasure of some accomplishment in the early beginning of my research career. Such incidences were repeated again when I published my papers on Holey carbon films for electron microscopy, new technique of contact electron micrography, moisture hysteresis studies on wheat seeds and structure-property relationships in native cotton a few years later in career. Today, the revolution in computer and Internet communication technology providing a direct access to the journals online and option to secretly download copies of the articles on your computer terminals, though marvelous has killed that emotional feel of being appreciated or admired for your research contribution by another scientist from a distant land that was felt on receiving the reprint request post-cards. Despite public funding of most of the research output in the world, excessive commercialization and greed for money is holding back the published research results for decades from the reach of a common researcher who has urge, desire and eagerness but no financial resources. Even public libraries are restricting access to literature without payment. The newer restrictions imposed by GATT, WTO and Intellectual Property Right (IPR) have more than vitiated the otherwise friendly, knowledge sharing, open and cooperative atmosphere in laboratories across the world and encouraged tendencies for secrecy, sabotage, suppression of genuine research findings, falsification and fabrication of research findings for ulterior motifs and piracies of all kinds. This is understandable to some extent in the event of a stiff competition for priority on research being independently pursued by various groups. But in general, if knowledge had not been shared globally in the historical past, humanity would never have progressed to the level it has done until the dawn of the 21 st century. I personally feel, publishers of research journals must allow free access to articles after three to five years from the date of publication. The third spectrophotometer method for trace determination of phosphorus that I was instrumental in developing, however, remained unpublished in view of my selection and joining the post of Assistant Physicist (Electron Microscopy) in 1971.

24

Beginning of the Science of Remote Sensing for Agriculture in India

Dr. C. Dakshinamutri in 1970 initiated studies and applications of aerial photography using infrared sensitive photographic films under a joint NASA-ISRO-IARI collaborative program; so as to catch spectral signatures of disease infected crops / trees on the ground in accordance with the fundamental principles of spectroscopy. He selected coastal areas of Kerala State in Southern India, known for prevalent infestation of coconut plantations with root wilt disease. I was asked to run the micro-densitometry tracings from the infrared photographic negatives exposed from over coconut groves with a 'Hasselblad camera' and map the intensity fluctuations. Little did I realize at that time as to what was all that about? But I soon came to know that I had unconsciously and unknowingly contributed to something pioneering in the country. Dr. Dakshinamurti had clearly detected signatures of coconut groves and trees infected with coconut root wilt disease after confirmation from ground truth observations and laid thereby the foundation for the science of 'Remote Sensing' and applications in agriculture in India and later in natural resource management. Today, Remote Sensing and its applications has become an essential major programme of priority under the aegis of the national and state government space agencies and space images are being extensively used in resource monitoring, planning, management and quality governance. It was again my privilege and honour to screen both purified and unpurified sample preparations of infected coconut plants from the field and also from healthy plants inoculated with cell saps of infected plants in transmission electron microscope in 1972-73 with Dr. A. S. Summanwar after I had joined the post of Assistant Physicist (Electron Microscopy). We repeated sample preparations with fresh inoculations of healthy plants under sterile glass house conditions and every time, detected rod shaped virus particles to be present in the samples and held responsible for the cause of root wilt disease. However, no conclusive identification was reached on the vector of this virus until that time. Here, I neither craved nor claimed any credit in the publications that followed.

The Science and technology of 'Remote Sensing' and applications in the management of natural resources of the country has grown into gigantic multi-level organizations under the Indian Space Research Organization and in various Units under the Central and individual State Governments.

25

Entering into the Microscopic World

My selection for electron microscopy literally pushed me into an entirely new world- 'the micro universe'. It is here, I realized the unimaginable dimensions of human knowledge from $\mathbf{10^{28}}$ cm in the outer cosmos to $\mathbf{10^{-14}}$ cm in the microscopic universe. Both these dimensions are beyond the un-aided human eye and only light in the form of electromagnetic energy connects the two extremes with the help of two complementary instruments; the telescope and the microscope. Here again, I was happy to have been selected for the post by none other than Dr. Kanwar Bahadur, a celebrated scientist from the Defense Research Laboratory and one of the first few pioneers in transmission electron microscopy in the country. Personally I had no familiarity with electron microscope beyond some theoretical introduction as part of my physics training and again it was a new challenge in my career. However, with an intention to usefully train a raw hand like me, Mr. Nam Prakash meticulously got all specimen preparations done through me under close personal observation, supervision and guidance. No wonder within shortest possible time, I not only learnt the science and art of specimen preparative techniques prevalent in those times, for observation in electron microscope, but even learnt to operate the transmission electron microscope and innovating techniques. It is during this phase, I learnt to keep my cool and patience and cultivate habit of reading as much as possible about the specimen being prepared for electron microscopy and about the very system of which it formed a part before concluding observations on the specimen. This was essential because of the limitations of specimen preparative techniques and subjective possibility of unconsciously introducing artifacts at molecular levels in microscopic structures. Mr. Nam Prakash used to teach a specialized course on Electron Microscopy to the post graduate students of the institute and he encouraged me to attend his classes, learn the science of electron microscopy and later allowed me to share his classroom lectures and practical classes as instructor. My foray into electron microscopy consciously or unconsciously brought me face to face with biological objects, their structures and interactions with energies of various kinds. The study of the small scale structure of matter (made possible by electron microscope and X-Rays) has been of immense value in discovering the secrets of life. I had no option left but to learn, understand biological cells, their structures, organelles, their functions and mutual interrelations, response to environmental conditions, to invasion by pathogens and viruses, physiological, metabolic changes initiated with such interactions and nutritional conditions during plant growth and interpretation of electron micrographs. However, the interpretation of electron micrographs is not an easy task and demands not only experience of years but basic knowledge and training for thinking in a multidisciplinary mode with capability to focus consciousness to perceive things at molecular and atomic dimensions. My training in physics was certainly advantageous in picking up things fast.

26

Green Revolution, Controversies and Turmoil in IARI

The period 1965 to 1972 was eventful in the history of the country and IARI in particular in that the fruits of the large changes in infrastructure, availability of fertilizers, electric power, irrigation facilities, and introduction of fertilizer-responsive Mexican dwarf wheat varieties bred by Norman E. Borlaug in the fields of Punjab, Haryana and Uttar Pradesh were visibly showing spectacular results. Grain harvest had surged to levels found never before and the country built a sizeable buffer stock of food grains for the first time. The proverbial 'green revolution' had practically ushered in and India soon stopped importing food grains from outside. It was my fortune to be a passive witness from inside to the developments beyond 1968 and fiercest battles between titans for credit to the success of green revolution. I was also a physical witness of all the contributors involved in the process of drafting and printing of the 'Young Scientist' Bulletin of the Association of Scientific Workers of India exposing the falsified data and claim by a high placed breeder's wheat protein controversy, the slanderously heated chorus by the unconcerned, unknown and ill-known scientists, orchestrated in defense of the concerned breeder in the institute auditorium, how the contributors involved in the drafting of the 'Young Scientist' bulletin suddenly and mysteriously turned their sides, and a roaring undeterred single handed, resolute attack exposing falsified wheat protein claims with evidence by Professor Y. V. Kathavate, Professor of Agricultural Physics in the institute and the student of Sir C. V. Raman (NL). The situation was saved with the outbreak of war with Pakistan in December 1971 and subsequent developments relegated the issue almost permanently in the background from the point of scientific ethics and morality, despite some international ramifications. Dr. A. B. Joshi, who played a crucial role in the reorganization of the ICAR and building infrastructure to bring about the developments, was called back in the middle of his FAO assignment by the Union Minister for Agriculture, to take charge of the post of Director General of ICAR. However, in surprisingly dramatic developments Dr. M. S. Swaminathan then Director-IARI was abruptly installed as the DG-ICAR and Dr. A. B. Joshi, who returned to India in response to the call from the President of ICAR was persuaded to take over as the Director of the Indian Agricultural Research Institute in 1972 until his retirement in 1977. Other memorable events that rocked the institute during my service period being a spate of suicides by scientists, institution of Justice P. B. Gajendragadkar Commission of Enquiry, the constitution of the Agricultural Research Service (ARS) of the ICAR and the long drawn struggle, demonstrations, street marches and sit-in-strikes by the In-Service scientists of ICAR for automatic induction into ARS, revised pay structures, scales and service conditions offered. It was a sad affair for me to witness and even participate in such street demonstrations despite fellow scientists being holding the top management positions in the ICAR; it was surprising why the genuine demands of the in-service scientists could not have been accepted by the authorities at the first instance? What was the wisdom in forcing strikes, demonstrations, disruptions in research and teaching activities and precious loss of man-hour productivity?

27

Lunch Hour Discussions and Scientific Pursuit

We, in the electron microscope unit **(Fig.10)** after our transfer to the newly established Nuclear Research Laboratory (NRL), formed a voluntary lunch-hour group for discussing scientific problems and issues; critically analyze the possible approaches to solve them without heirchical subservience or authoritative dominance.

Figure 10: Electron Microscope Group of N.R.L.
Front row (L to R) Mr. Nam Prakash, Dr. Sushil Kumar and Dr. A. V. Moharir. Back row: Mr. Vijay Kumar Sharma, Mr. Ved Prakash Upadhyaya and Mr. Jagat Singh

Though relatively junior in age and position, even my views were heard with due respect and attention. And our lunch hour group **(Fig.10)** included stalwarts as; Dr. Sushil Kumar, a bacterial geneticist and a S. S. Bhatnagar Prize awardee; Dr. B. C. Panda, a physicist and philosopher; Dr. B. R. Murti, a geneticist, biometrician and also a S. S. Bhatnagar Prize awardee; Dr. M. W. Hardas, a geneticist and a pioneer in plant introduction; Dr. S. L. Mehta a biochemist; Dr. S. Bhaskaran, a somatic cell geneticist; Dr. M. G. Joshi, Breeder and geneticist; Dr. Anupan Varma, a plant virologist; Dr. S. K. Ghosh, a soil clay mineralogist; Dr. K. N. Mehrotra, insect physiologist and Dr. N. Ramakrishnan, an insect pathologists; Dr. A. C. Gaur, Dr. S. K. Kavimandan, Dr. S. T. Shende and Dr. I. Eshwaran and Dr. A. R. Varma, microbiologists, besides several others who frequently came from other ICAR institutes for electron microscopy assistance would join us for interaction.

Figure 11: Lunch hour group (L to R) Mr. Nam Prakash, Dr. Sushil Kumar and Dr. A. V. Moharir

Several Trained Engineers from M/S Philips India, who used to visit the laboratory on routine or emergency service, also provided me with most practical tips on maintenance and operation of the microscope which they had acquired from their own training in Holland, through such lunch hour discussions. They also provided me with copies of the booklets produced by the Electron Microscopy Applications Laboratory of Philips, Holland. I was also invited and sponsored for a day long visit to this laboratory in Eindhoven in Holland during my European Commission fellowship in Ghent-Belgium. It was here, I was surprised to find the Philips laboratory technicians to be using 'carbon holey films' for correction of astigmatism in electron microscope lenses, prepared according to the technique developed by me and Nam Prakash.

It was during one such lunch-hour meeting, almost prophetically, I had pointed out to Dr. B. R. Murti (*Project Director, NRL*) as to how my research on structure-property relationships in native cotton fibres on all the four commercial species (*described separately*) was significant for the twenty first century. It was then in 1986, in one of my comprehensive research paper, I had given an emphatic call to change our cotton breeding priority from 'breeding for increased staple length' to 'breeding for increased tensile strength of fibres'. This was essential in view of the emergence of fast, efficient, Open-End-Spinning technology and its demand of higher tensile strength as the first requisite on raw cotton fibre properties over staple length. How I wish, we had recorded these discussions in those hours. They were intensive and scholarly interactions on various subjects with occasional deep, in-sighted inputs from physicists like Mr. Nam Prakash, known for his penetrating ability to seek instant correlations. These colleagues from the field of agriculture realized the importance and enjoyed the value of discussing their problems with us physicists and got new clues for solving their own problems. No wonder, all of them produced some innovative original research individually and with their students, won recognition and laurels and occupied important positions of authority. And they include Dr. G. S. Venkatraman, Dr. N. S. Subbarao, Dr. Sushil Kumar, Dr. K. N. Mehrotra, Dr. N. Ramakrishnan, Dr. B. R. Murti, Dr. Anupam Varma, Dr. S. L. Mehta, Dr. S. K. Sinha, Dr. M. L. Lodha and several others. I do not know how Mr. Nam Prakash got to develop such uncanny penetrating ability, but I feel very strongly that his training as an elementary particle physicist concerned with dimensions from $\mathbf{10^{-14}}$ to $\mathbf{10^{28}}$ cm, encompassing the material world from elementary particles to the cosmic universe and his deep spiritual practice in meditation in the 'Radha Saomi (Dayal Bagh, Agra) faith' was the fundamental under-current behind his comprehension of the micro and macro universe. This is also demonstrative of the fact how knowledge of Physics and Physical laws help us in our comprehension of any problem from any disciplines of science.

28

Establishment of the Nuclear Research Laboratory and Transfer to NRL

A characteristic feature of the developments in physical and applied physical sciences, particularly in the last two hundred years are the unlimited energy options made available to mankind and these have destroyed the artificially erected boundaries between different chapters of natural sciences[2]. No wonder, chemical reactions, biological processes, phenomena of the inanimate world are now being studied by the same methods and techniques and proceed from common theoretical premises. Physical laws are therefore the undercurrent of all creations in the universe as the 'Unified Field' is believed to be the only source behind the physical universe and all creations on the surface of the earth.

Under the process of the reorganization and restructuring the Indian Council of Agricultural Research (ICAR), the research and development activities at the institute were moving in top gear. A new multidisciplinary laboratory, called Nuclear Research Laboratory (NRL) **(Fig.12)** was established in 1969 as a National facility for research, use and training human resource, with financial assistance from the United Nations Development Program for plant-biological research at cellular and sub-cellular levels using stable and radio isotope tracer and physical nuclear techniques.

Figure 12: The Nuclear Research Laboratory (N.R.L.) Established in 1969

Conceptually, the NRL represented a finest example of foresighted thought of integrating physical science and analytical physical techniques in agricultural research and probe reasons for improvement of quality, traits and productivity of various crop plants at molecular levels and their correlations with structure and genetic make up. Dr. C. Dakshinamurti, played a key role in drawing the blue-print and infrastructure plan for the NRL by putting sophisticated precision physical instruments and growth chambers for artificially controlled environmental conditions for growing experimental plants under one roof. These facilities were backed up by very strong multidisciplinary groups of researchers in physics, biochemistry, plant-physiology, plant-pathology, entomology, somatic cell genetics, soil mineralogy and fertility with a basic objective of carrying out collaborative research to understand the physical processes that control plant growth and yield and possibly evolve new technologies for sustainable crop production.

A whole range of sophisticated instruments were procured and installed under one roof and these included X-Ray diffractometer, Nuclear Magnetic Resonance Spectrometer, Transmission electron microscope, Mass spectrometer, Liquid scintillation counter, Multichannel analyzer, a fully equipped radio isotope laboratory for research and training human resource, Gamma cell for irradiation of biological specimens for enhanced shelf-life, inducing mutations, sterilization of insects populations and several others. It was again my privilege and honour to design an emblem for the Nuclear Research Laboratory that depicted almost all profile of its research activities and mandate so precisely and my design of a conical flask containing a vertical germinated plant from its seed and roots below at the centre of the flask with three cross oriented electron orbits surrounding it was officially adopted on the eve of the Silver Jubilee function of the laboratory in 1994 and became the component of the souvenir plates in brass released and distributed on the occasion **(Fig.13, a, b& c).**

Dr. P. N. Tiwari
Project Director

Nuclear Research Laboratory
Indian Agricultural Research Instt .
New Delhi , 110 012 , India

Dated : 13-2-1989

CERTIFICATE

This is to certify that the accompanying emblem has been designed by Dr. A. V. Moharir and that the same was incorporated on the title page of the bulletin of this laboratory highlighting the research contributions since its establishment in 1969 .

P.N. Tiwari
(P. N. Tiwari)

Figure 13 (a, b, c): a. Emblem for N.R.L.; b. Certificate; c. Emblem as printed on Silver Jubilee Souvenir Brass Plates

Scientists from the NRL were deputed abroad for training and wider exposure in modern scientific researches in respective fields using stable and radio isotopes and nuclear techniques. In an attempt to provide sharper focus to the research projects, the transmission electron microscope unit from the Division of Agricultural Physics was transferred to the Nuclear Research Laboratory along with men and equipment and I became a member of the Nuclear Research Laboratory in 1971 and returned back to the Division of Agricultural Physics after 28 years in 1999 as Professor. My transfer to the NRL aroused a hope that I shall also be deputed abroad in the normal process for a formal training which I lacked in use and applications of electron microscope. But that was not to be because the component of the budget allocation towards training in electron microscopy was intentionally diverted by Dr. N. P. Datta, the then Project Director for purchase of other instruments, despite the fact that a more versatile high resolution equipment, Philips EM-300 Transmission Electron Microscope had already been purchased for the laboratory. I was even assigned the responsibility of transporting the EM-consignments from the warehouse in Bombay Docks (Now Mumbai) to New Delhi and later be involved in its installation and commission at the NRL with the engineers from the Philips India company. Undisturbed, with the diversion of funds meant for our professional training abroad for other use, both me and Nam Prakash resolved to perform to our best with self learning and personal experience. Thanks to the engineers from the local Philips India office who regularly posted us with the latest technical bulletins from their EM-Applications Laboratory in Holland. Also with support from the institute librarians, I managed to build a sizeable collection of latest reference books, advances, monographs, conference proceedings and other texts on electron microscopy and applications in biological and material sciences besides subscribing important journals in the institute library to keep ourselves abreast with developments. I am particularly grateful to successive librarians; Late Mr. S. P. Phadnis, Mr Shoib Hassan, Mr. Chhotey Lal and Mr. N. S. Pakhale for their appreciating our difficulty, understanding, cooperation and going out of their priorities, despite constrains on their budget for library acquisitions in foreign exchange. They all religiously lived the lives of spirited professional librarian with genuine concern for the scientists and scientific progress. Their cooperation helped me and my colleague Mr. Nam Prakash to keep ourselves abreast with the progress and developments in the field of electron microscopy and remain competitive all through our service life. Both Mr. Nam Prakash and myself, never ever felt dejected for being denied a formal training abroad in the area of our pursuit. In fact this decision helped both of us to be self-reliant and confident to tread our own paths. There was immense pleasure for both of us in learning through self efforts. I felt the immense joy of such independent self-efforts when I forwarded a copy of my published paper on the new technique of 'Contact Electron Micrography' to Sir Ernst Ruska (NL), the co-inventor of Transmission Electron Microscope with Max Knoll, and received in return, a copy of his 'Nobel Lecture' along with a copy of his self-autographed photo. It was during the directorship of Dr. B. R. Murti in 1977, I was deputed to undergo training in the use of stable and radio isotopes and nuclear techniques in agriculture at the Timiryazev Agricultural Academy, Moscow-USSR on a fellowship from the International Atomic Energy Agency and also Mr. Nam Prakash to the same country on a short visit.

The Nuclear Research Laboratory reverberated with vibrant research and training activities as long as the funds were flowing from the UNDP and later from the Swedish International Development Authority (SIDA). The Government of India failed to sustain the activities of NRL at optimum levels beyond commitment by SIDA, in providing matching grants on its own to update the obsolete capital-intensive instrumental facilities. The appointments for the post of Project Director of NRL, despite specially constituted committees of renowned experts for selection, right from the beginning, were mired into wars of influences. In my personal considered opinion, as an insider, witness to the developments and participant in the activities, the conceptually beautiful, sophisticated multidisciplinary Nuclear Research Laboratory never got the right kind of person to head it from its beginning, despite the fact that all those selected were brilliant in their own areas of specialty and contribution to science. The very concept of NRL as a multidisciplinary application laboratory to study the fundamental process in plants genetics, understanding and improvement or transformation using nuclear and allied techniques demanded uniquely unconventional abilities on the part of its director with capacity to hybridize ideas from one discipline to other, visualize linkages, build teams for focused objective and correlate observations for an integrated holistic look at the problems in hand. Whereas, the founder Project Director could never appreciate the specific essential requirements of a dust-free, dark laboratory space for electron microscopic observation and so much to even deny a dedicated photographic dark-room facility for developing and printing of micrographs despite counseling. His successor, a renowned biometrician and geneticist was practically ignorant about physical nuclear instruments and their potentials for research. But he was honest, very sharp and aware of his weakness. He used to invite Mr. Nam Prakash and sometimes me to brief him about physical instruments before taking any decision. On one occasion, he asked Nam Prakash and me to give exclusive lectures to him on electron microscopy, its potential and use at a stretch for almost three hours. Soon, thereafter, amazingly enough, he himself drafted M.Sc. and Ph.D. theses programs for three of his students on cytogenetic studies of male sterility in pearl millet, based exclusively on ultra-structural investigation using transmission electron microscope.

Unfortunately, the only physicist who headed NRL for thirteen long years was ineffective in drawing any project funds from national or international funding agencies for upgrading instrumental facilities. The others in continuation, who officiated as project directors were only occasional users of stable or radio-isotopes as tracers in their studies. No wonder, a unique, sophisticated, multidisciplinary Nuclear Research Laboratory should have gradually turned merely into a place of out-dated instrumental facilities within three decades from its establishment. It is unfortunate that the government could not sustain and maintain this unique laboratory for long even for fundamental academic work in plant genetics at cellular levels. I am not sure if the example of the Nuclear Research Laboratory, represents a convincing demonstration of the prophetic opinion expressed by Lord Ernest Rutherford (NL), the creator of Nuclear Physics, shortly before his death that-he was convinced that no large scale applications of nuclear physics would ever occur? Even so, I personally feel confident that large multidisciplinary groups of scientists could have been assembled to integrate problems of fundamental basic importance around every sophisticated high resolution physical instrument, such as Transmission and Scanning Electron Microscopes, Nuclear Magnetic Resonance Spectrometer, X-Ray diffractometer, Mass Spectrometer and Gamma Cell, with mandate to produce standard reference data catalogues on structural characteristic and morphological features of micro-flora, insects, pests, soil clay minerals, etc. for the country. The absence of these was clearly missed by the scientists during interpretation of research results on samples drawn from within the country. We had no option but to often refer to 'American standard catalogues' for clues and support in identification and interpretation. Another major reason, as I personally feel very strongly for failure in strengthening NRL being that scientists were raising crop plants in pots, fields or in growth chambers as per their personal interests. They were never asked to draw their samples for whatever individual problem of study they were interested in; from one common single crop type, grown on same farm, same crop season under uniform agro-climatic conditions and pool research data from all investigations (In relation to biochemical, physiological, biophysical, genetics, structural, soil chemical and plant nutritional angles etc.) for inter-parameter, interdisciplinary correlative studies for seeking some fundamental insight. This kind of collective approach would have helped to not only develop technologies for efficient crop production and quality in respect of individual crop types over the years but also fundamental understanding on individual crop plant type at cellular and molecular levels.

29

Training in Multidisciplinary Approach to Problems

It is in the NRL, I had my intensive training, interactions and comprehension of diverse problems of agricultural research and approach in a multidisciplinary way. It is here, I truly understood the importance, relevance, depth, power and necessity of learning or knowing physics and physical laws as an under current of all problems in biology and agriculture. The superfluous nature of boundaries between disciplines, drawn and erected by those who dared not to venture into areas of investigation other than their own was truly realized. After all, there is nothing else in the entire biological and non-biological universe other than inter-play of matter and energies of various kinds and their mutual interactions that constitutes an essential part of training in physics. It is in the NRL, I realized the realities of drastic changes induced on growth and health of plants at the molecular, structural and morphological levels and their vulnerability to apparently insignificant fluctuations of environmental temperature, humidity, light, nutrition and moisture. Thanks to the various multidisciplinary research projects to which I was associated with, discussions with colleagues and inputs they provided in interpretation of microscopic structures for giving me the capacity for a holistic approach to problems and penetrating depth in thinking. The current out cry from all those who understand the seriousness of the consequences of human tampering of global environment on food security for billions of human beings on the earth is therefore fully justified. No wonder, in anticipation of the likely consequences of our past actions, large pools of germplasm of all categories of crop plants have been collected, frozen and meticulously stored in our 'gene banks' for possible future use in breeding new genotypes as per demand. However, the commercial greed, obsession for making quick ransom money (through sale of preserved genetic stock) and ownership rights have made such collections from gene banks almost inaccessible for poor farmers except by the corporate seed agencies and multinational seed companies. The fear of losing all we have for survival on the Earth is not unreal. This has now been acknowledged with acceptance of the final report of the Inter Governmental Panel on Climate Change (IPCC) and the award of the Nobel Prize to this committee. The increasing pollution and artificial loading of nitrous oxides in atmosphere have already been documented to be responsible for vanishing biodiversity at alarming rates. The greatest agricultural scientist of modern India, Late Dr. A. B. Joshi, in expressing his anguish against commercialization of plant variety collections and deposits in gene banks, had rightly said ***(Reference-17)*** in no uncertain words- “A frozen bank account is of no value to its depositors if it is not made freely available / accessible”. In the first ever published report on depletion of atmospheric nitrogen, I have brought out recently the seriousness of withdrawing atmospheric nitrogen for production of fertilizer and industrial applications in ever increasing quantities annually, to be more catastrophic than relatively small increase or decrease in concentration of other green house gases in the atmosphere ***(Reference-11).***

30

Taking Roots in the Science of Electron Microscopy

Some interesting experiments

- ***Problem with Formvar specimen support films and high resolution test specimens***

Essential spares, supplies, chemicals for running an electron microscope facility had to be all imported from abroad. And in view of the scarcity of foreign exchange, and in an attempt to keep the approved research projects going on uninterrupted, we had to be judicious in taking up any additional work. Three pieces of copper grids coated with holey carbon films, essentially required for correcting astigmatism in electron lenses were costing around fifty US dollars, without guarantee that these could be reused. These difficulties prompted me to reduce our dependence on foreign supplies and to develop my own method of preparing holey carbon films as test specimens for correcting astigmatism and nets for mounting specimens for high resolution microscopy. I used simple physical principles and physical properties of heats of vaporization, specific heats, boiling point, specific gravity, surface tension and solubility of two commonly used solvents, ethylene dichloride and chloroform for dissolving 'Formvar' (poly-vinyl formaldehyde) polymer used for casting support films for mounting EM-specimens. The developed method was not only simple, reproducible and effective but could help produce holes of any size from few Angstrom to few microns in diameter. My paper describing my technique was immediately accepted for publication in the Journal of Physics (E) Scientific Instruments and my electron micrograph of nets was published on the cover page of the issue of the journal in which this article appeared. It is my consolation that even four decades after publication, this paper still enjoys citations.

- ***Contact electron micrography a new technique***

Scarcity of foreign exchange for importing essential supplies and spares prompted me to look for local substitutes without compromising on quality and accuracy of results. It is in this process, out of curiosity and to compare and contrast the characteristics of locally available filter paper with the expensive 'Whatman Grade' paper imported for routine use,

I did an innovative experiment in recording electron micrographs of various grades of filter papers held tightly in contact with photographic film plates and using the conventional plate camera system of the transmission electron microscope. The results were surprising enough to reproduce and estimate the pore sizes of the various grades of filter paper to given accuracy. This established the birth of a new technique of 'contact electron micrography' for characterization of paper and such other thin film materials for composition, uniformity, thickness variations and other properties. The paper was immediately accepted and published in the Journal of Materials Science. Whereas one may ask, what has this to do with agricultural research? And I must stress that it was the absolute academic freedom that the scientists in the Indian Agricultural Research Institute enjoyed that enabled me to do something more and different from the routine research projects. Besides, it was my open mind and inherent curiosity that urged me to spend extra hours in the laboratory and pursue innovative experiments. After all, it is always the first step that is responsible for a giant leap ahead. History of science and technology is replete with several such examples.

- ***Collodion blended Formvar specimen support films***

Difficulties were being experienced in mounting particulate clay minerals and purified plant and insect virus specimens in that the virus particles and the aqueous solutions of electron stains were not getting uniformly spread over pure Formvar substrates in view of the hydrophobic nature of these films. Observation and characterization of individual virus particle was often difficult in that they would coalesce together and get embedded in the matrix of the electron dense stain. This difficulty prompted me to attempt blending of hydrophobic Formvar with hydrophilic Collodion (nitrocellulose) polymer in a common solvent and then cast blended support films. The experiment was so successful that with a calibrated amount of Collodion blended with Formvar, I could produce specimen support films that had the hydrophilic nature of Collodion and strength of Formvar to withstand the intense electron beam temperature and ensured uniform spread of both electron stain and virus specimens for observation in electron microscope. Both the holey and blended films were proved to be boon in practical electron microscopy and are still in vogue and popular with microscopists all over the world.

- ***Positively stained shadow cast insect virus specimens for simultaneous revelation of internal details and surface morphology contours***

The field of electron microscopy even in the eighties was open to innovation as every individual specimen presented its own problems for observation in the microscope because of the limitation on specimen thickness, extreme vacuum within the microscope column and generation of high temperature within specimen from the interaction with electron beam. Therefore, there was ample scope for unconsciously introducing, distortions / artifacts to specimen during sample preparation and these were revealed only on observation in the microscope. No wonder specimen preparation for transmission electron microscopy was both a science and an art. In this process, my early attempts to deposit heavy metal (shadow cast) under vacuum over positively stained insect virus; Nuclear Polyhedrosis Virus (NPV) specimens were genuinely successful. Whereas positive staining revealed the internal details of the viral DNA coil, shadow casting with gold-palladium revealed details on the surfaces of the individual virus particles. It was an exciting result. However, the grain size of our shadow cast gold-palladium alloy material was relatively very large and it would have been a difficult task to convince or even expect the editors of any journal to perceive and see through my eyes, what I was trying to demonstrate. We did not possess 'Platinum-Carbon' rods as shadow cast material known for their very fine grain size at that time. I delayed publishing my results on shadow cast positively stained NPV viruses as a new technique until we receive our supply of Pt-Carbon and repeat the experiment for clear unambiguous micrographs on the advice of my senior colleague but very soon lost priority to others.

- ***Carbon surface replicas of relatively large sized rock specimens***

It was during this time, our collaboration and help was sought from scientists from the Geology department of Delhi University in their study of rock samples collected from the Kotdwara region of Garhwal District in the Himalayas. Scanning Electron Microscopes had not yet arrived in India in large numbers and easily available and the only possible mean of studying the surface features of rock samples at high resolution in electron microscope was by preparing their surface replicas in plastic moulds or in vacuum evaporated carbon films deposited over rock samples and subsequently dissolving the sample material in suitable solvents. The energy and rate of reaction in dissolution of sample often ruptured or distorted the replica moulds and certainly needed some innovative means to avoid them. It is here; I attempted to deposit evaporated carbon under vacuum from below with simultaneous rotation of specimen at 100 rpm and holding them inclined to around 40-45 ^{0} angles to the vertical. The idea was to deposit carbon within all cavities of the primary impression of the specimen in polymer film above, a uniform layer of evaporated carbon deposit. Having deposited such carbon films within the cavities of the impressions, the polymer films were dissolved in suitable solvent leaving the carbon surface replicas of rock grains behind. Surface features of rock specimens as large as 4-5 mm in size could be successfully replicated using this procedure. The technical method and results were soon published in Current Science.

- ***Extreme vacuum desiccation of wheat seeds and their viability***

Biological materials including seeds are known to constantly absorb and desorbs moisture at room temperature. Seeds in particular, loose their viability over time, specific to their species, structure and biochemical composition. And in general, excessive moisture absorption or storage under uncontrolled humid conditions, seed of all types are known to degenerate in quality, germination and viability besides suffer enhanced invasion by insects, micro flora and pathogens. Water molecules however, are known to play a vital role in maintaining the structural integrity and functional viability of seeds as a continuing genetic material as a part of the composition of the seed material usually referred as the 'bound water' in scientific terminology. Generally, considerable amount of energy is required to remove bound water from the structural composition and this amount of energy is different for different biological materials and seeds. There are several ways of removing structural bound water and heating is perhaps the most efficient and definitive. Vacuum desiccation is another method to remove moisture from the seeds and it was my curiosity to find out the extent of time and order of vacuum desiccation, seeds of wheat varieties of different species can withstand without loss in germination and viability. While I was toying with such ideas, it just happened that for some administrative reasons in importing an essential spare part, our electron microscope was out of operation for a sustained period. I found it to be the best opportune time for running a preliminary experiment on vacuum desiccation of wheat seeds of different varieties and species using our vacuum coating unit that could evacuate up to 10^{-7} Torr of mercury pressure. Several seed lots of wheat were desiccated for various intervals from 2 to 12 hours at a stretch at 10^{-7} Torr of mercury pressure and subjected to germination over wet whatman grade filter paper in Petri plates. Germination percent was computed for varieties of all species for all durations of desiccation times. It was surprising to see no deterioration in germination even after 12 hours of desiccation of seeds at such low pressure. Growth of plantlets in all treatments was studied for over ten days and observed significant faster development from desiccated seeds as compared to control but gradually the difference leveled off. One thing remarkable being that seeds desiccated for 10 and 12 hours were observed to had two leaves coming out from split developing radical on germination instead of one as in the normal case from almost 30-40% of the desiccated seeds. My desire to take these studies up to grain formation and maturity stages of the plant growth could not be fulfilled on account of other commitments and priorities. It is here, I lamented my helplessness in not being given any student to guide for M.Sc despite being a faculty member of the discipline of Agricultural Physics since 1971. Such short-term problems could have been ideal for the student's theses work. They had a potential to be developed into big entrepreneur industries, possible for consumption or use in the space technology missions of today.

- ***Desiccation and moisture regain studies on cotton fibres***

Use of vacuum coating unit for desiccation of wheat seeds and a Marconi digital moisture meter available in the laboratory, prompted me also to study moisture regain characteristics of various cotton varieties of different species, which I had collected as pure breeder's material for my own studies. Moisture hysteresis curves plotted for fibres of different varieties and species revealed inherent differences and could have been correlated to the amount of cellulose synthesized and deposited within the matrix of fibres during their growth on plants. This study, though interesting could not be pursued to its logical end for want of time and compulsions of attending to the committed work on priority. However, this could have been a thesis problem for any post graduate student with important consequences for practical applications in cotton processing.

- ***Carbon support films directly cast over glass or mica sheets***

It is common knowledge that different organic liquids burn at different rates and deposit sooty carbon films over substrates held horizontal over the flame. The thickness of the deposited film depends upon the size of the flame, time of deposit and rate of burning. Since carbon films are known to have very poor adhesion with glass surfaces and more so with freshly cleaved mica sheets, it was my curiosity to find out if such films deposited by burning organic liquids can be suitably substituted for the vacuum evaporated carbon films for mounting specimens for observation under electron microscope? I borrowed a metallic laboratory burner from a nearby senior secondary school, inserted a fresh cotton wick tightly over its nose and verified first in the open space, if various organic liquids could be safely burnt with a flame for short intervals of time without causing explosion. Carbon films of various thicknesses were cast over mica substrates from benzene, carbon tetrachloride and liquid paraffin. These carbon films in view of their poor adhesion with mica sheet surfaces could be easily floated on water in a bowl and even mounted over copper support grid meshes. However, on observation under electron microscope, it was realized that such carbon films were indeed themselves amorphous to the electron beam, but were invariably superimposed with long chains of carbon deposits, something similar to the 'Fullerenes' as we know now. The use of such carbon films from burning organic liquids was therefore out of question for our purpose for obvious reasons and the experiment was not pursued further. *(Fullerenes are a form of carbon molecules that is neither graphite nor diamond but consist of spherical, ellipsoid or cylindrical arrangement of dozens of carbon atoms)*

The above descriptions of small experiments have been mentioned, only to indicate that there was ample freedom and flexibility to a scientist in the institute (IARI) to explore new avenues and ideas, provided a scientist has the will to perform, inner urge for scientific curiosity and eagerness for exploring the unknown in search of some thing new. At the same time, we as scientists were never asked to take a commercial look at our research or seek patents nor encouraged enough to independently submit project proposals for funding and resources from out side the institute. Situation changed suddenly only after 1980 and onward after reports about GATT, WTO and IPR related issues came into circulation. Under such situations, it certainly was an honest effort on my part to at least remain engaged in exploration of new ideas one or the other dictated by the limitations of the known procedures at that time. After all, each new discovery or invention germinates from a 'seed idea' and the foundations of all major industries of today can be traced to such small beginnings by some one some where, working in isolation in a remote corner of an establishment, sacrificing his personal time and leisure in pursuit of crazy new ideas. These small experiments I conducted, may not have struck something very big or spectacular for me but certainly helped me in building up my capacity and boost self confidence. Nevertheless my new technique of 'Contact Electron Micrography' and concept of 'Normalized Moisture Hysteresis Curves' for screening wheat varieties suitable for rain-fed cultivation actually grew out of such experiments. It was this obsession that kept me engaged in the laboratory beyond usual working hours. I was only fortunate that my loving, understanding and cooperative wife and daughters never complained about my returning late at home and reposing full faith in my honest pursuits and integrity.

- ***Contribution to identify and characterize plant viruses specific to some plant diseases***

Working in close collaboration with scientists from the Divisions of Plant Pathology, Microbiology and Entomology, I was associated in identification and characterization of the viruses responsible for mosaic disease of musk melon *(cucumis melo-L)*, cowpea mosaic virus (*Vigna Sinensis savi)*, root wilt disease in coconut (TMV type rod shaped virus), *Spirilum lipoferum* bacteria in the stems of wheat plant, Mycoplasmal like bodies responsible for the Wich's Broom disease of cowpea and the Nuclear Polyhedrosis virus multiplied and isolated from the insect *Spodoptera litura*. Studies with viruses fascinated me so much that I sincerely thought of shifting myself full time in doing some Biophysical work at the cross roads of boundaries between physics and biology and to divert to the emerging subject of –'Biophysics of Viruses' and particularly on the origin and genesis of viruses. A suggestive proposal to this effect was made at the initiative and encouragement from Professor Anupam Varma and the stage was practically set for action when a new dedicated transmission electron microscope was installed in the Division of Plant Pathology. I had set two conditions before I accept my shifting; (1) that I shall be allowed an independent project on the biophysical aspects of plant viruses as leader and enjoy discretion in selecting or rejecting specimens / preparations for observation in the TEM as in-charge of the facility and (2) my annual assessment would be done in my parent discipline i.e. Physics and not in the Plant Pathology as I wanted to retain my basic identity as a physicist. However, for reasons not made known to me, my transfer to the Division of Plant Pathology could not actually take place and hope of initiating new work on 'Biophysics of Plant Viruses' died and remained a dream for the rest of the service period of my life.

31

Normalized Moisture Hysteresis Curves of Seeds: A New Concept

- ***Studies on moisture hysteresis in seeds of wheat varieties of different species:***

Every kind of plant biological material including seeds is known to continuously absorb and de-sorb moisture and remain in dynamic equilibrium with the environment at any moment of time. However the rate of absorption of moisture by any material is not equal to the rate of desorption and thereby exhibits this lag as a phenomenon known as the hysteresis. Hysteresis reveals information regarding many things hidden such as the structure and composition of the seed, permeability of the membranes involved, amount and quality of proteins, moisture holding capacity and amount of bound water that goes in holding the composition of the seed material intact together. In the magnetization of soft iron or an alloy material, hysteresis is known to play a very crucial role and area enveloped under the closed hysteresis loop is a direct measure of the energy required for magnetization and resistance offered by the material to magnetization. It was my curiosity to study the moisture analogue of magnetic hysteresis in seeds and possible linkage of such a phenomenon with genetic characteristics of varieties within and between species of wheat *(Triticum aestivum, Triticum durum and Triticum dicoccum).* Wetting and drying of seeds before sowing has been a regular practice with wheat farmers. This practice called 'priming' has been known to not only germinate seeds vigorously but also to produce a good stand of the crop. However, repeated cycles of 'priming' of seeds under natural or artificial high humidity conditions are also known to degenerate and reduce viability of seeds.

I decided to make use of an incubator, fitted with double doors and a precisely controlling temperature regulating thermostat for the purpose of my study. A preliminary experiment revealed that the incubator could build a stable 65% RH relative humidity conditions inside the chamber at 30.0^{0} Celsius temperature and seeds of wheat varieties came to saturation in about 12-14 hours at a stretch under these conditions. I decided to run my experiments with these boundary conditions and compare seed lots of varieties and species for possible clues for characterization. Considering huge inherent natural variability in biological materials, I also decided to run five sets of individual replications for each variety and then take the mean average value as a representative figure for the variety. For the sake of convenience, I decided to first bring the lots of wheat seeds in five replications to saturation at 30.0^0 Celcius and 65% RH and then observe the progress in dehydration at 30.0^0 Celcius by observing the loss in mass at regular intervals of 2.0 hours for next 12 hours. The seed lots were subjected to rehydration at 30.0^0 Celcius and 65% RH and progressive changes in the mass of seeds was observed at regular interval of 2.0 hours for next 12 hours. The Progressive loss in mass of seeds during dehydration and increase during re-hydration cycles were normalized and moisture hysteresis curves were established for each of the wheat varieties. Area enclosed between the hysteresis loops for individual varieties was measured both with a planimeter and also by counting from the square graph sheets. The study was deliberately kept confined to the varieties of wheat which had been officially released for cultivation after extensive trials under All India Coordinated Wheat Improvement Project and their production status; as a variety released for rain-fed cultivation or for irrigated cultivation or for both under rain-fed and irrigated cultivation was definitely known. The surprising observation was that; if varieties under investigation are arranged in the increasing order of the area enclosed under their hysteresis loops, all the well known and well established rain-fed varieties moved to the top of the table and the varieties released for irrigated cultivation moved to the bottom of the table and the varieties that have been released for cultivation under both rainfed and irrigated cultivation find a place somewhere in the middle of the table. Smaller area under the normalized moisture hysteresis loops therefore corresponds to the increased drought tolerant status of the wheat variety. This behaviour was observed to be true within varieties of all the three individual species of wheat; *Triticum aestivum, Triticum durum* and *Triticum dicoccum* **(Fig. 14 and Tables 1a and 1b).**

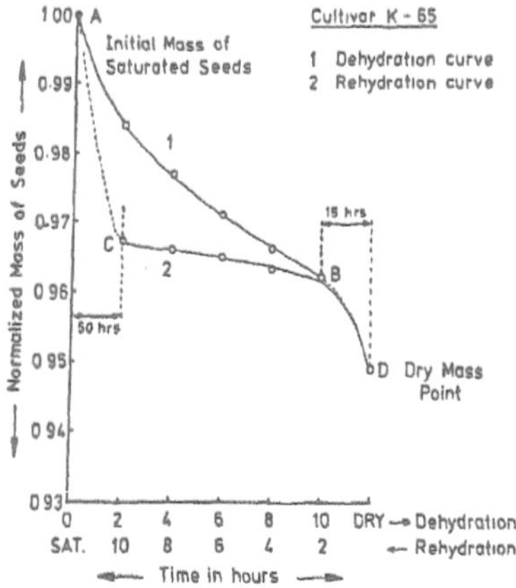

Figure 1. Normalized hysteresis curve for the wheat variety K-65

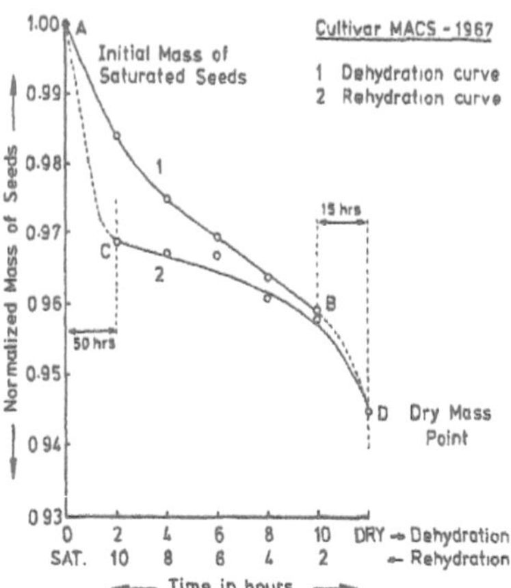

Figure 3. Normalized hysteresis curve for the wheat variety MACS-1967

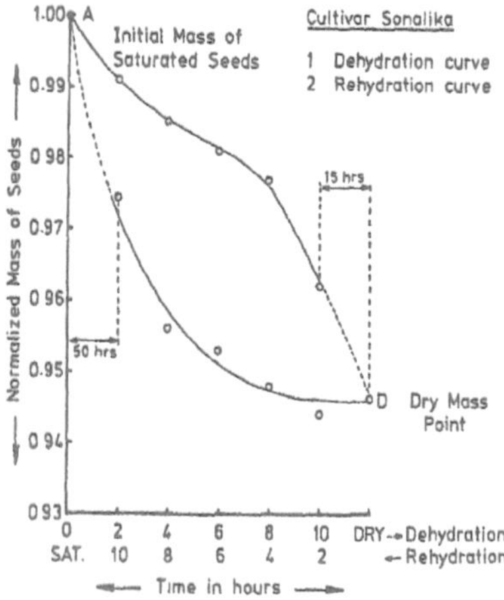

Figure 2. Normalized hysteresis curve for the wheat variety Sonalika.

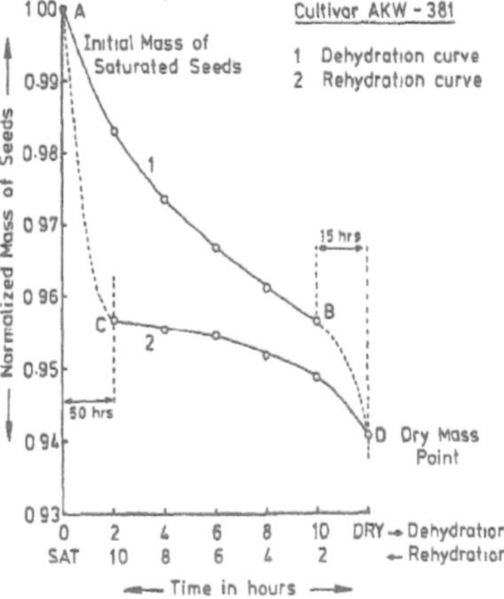

Figure 4. Normalized hysteresis curve for the wheat variety AKW-381

Figure 14: Typical Normalized Wheat Seed-Moisture Hysteresis Curves for varieties of *Triticum aestivum* and *Triticum durum*

Table 1a: Area of Normalized Moisture Hysteresis Loops in *T. aestivum* varieties and their agronomic production status

Sl. No.	Name of wheta variety	Agronomic production conditions (#)	Area under moisture hysteresis loop (cm^2)	Increase/decrease in hydration over conditioned seeds(%)	Moisture retention index
1.	K-65	TS-RF	19.36 (L)	(-) 0.616	8.01 (L)
2.	C-306	TS-RF	22.20 (L)	(-) 0.740 (L)	9.39
3.	K-8027	TS-RF	22.42	(-) 0.671	11.06
4.	WL-410	LS-RF	23.74	(-) 0.410	13.36
5.	Mukta	TS-RF	24.46	(-) 0.270	11.45
6.	WL-711	TS-IR	25.35	(+) 0.322	12.76
7.	WH-147	TS-IR	28.66	(-) 0.401	13.71
8.	K-8020	LS-IR	28.68	(-) 0.281	12.94
9.	DL-153-2	TS-RF	28.80	(-) 0.088	12.47
10.	NI-5439	TS-RF+IR	31.24	(+) 0.233	14.70
11.	K-68	TS+RF+IR	35.72	(+) 0.043	15.98
12.	IWP-72	TS-RF	38.80	(+) 0.466	21.56
13.	Kalyan-Sona	TS-IR	39.64	(+) 0.386	20.31
14.	HD-2009	TS-IR	42.50	(+) 0.658	21.38
15.	Sonalika	LS-IR	63.94	(+) 1.608	27.91
16.	HD-2329	TS-IR	64.14	(+) 0.994	27.65
17.	WH-157	TS-IR	65.70 (H)	(+) 1.805 (H)	28.22 (H)
18.	Range of variation (max.-min)		46.34	2.545	20.21

Table 1b: Area of Normalized Moisture Hysteresis Loops in *T. durum* varieties and their agronomic production status

Sl. No.	Name of wheta variety	Agronomic production conditions (#)	Area under moisture hystĕresis loop (cm^2)	Increase/decrease in hydration over conditioned seeds(%)	Moisture retention index
1.	AKW-1811	New genotypes TS-IR	15.25 (L)	(-) 0.9300	8.49
2.	AKW-1071	TS-IR	15.86	(-) 0.9662 (L)	8.14
3.	NP-404	TS-RF	16.14	(-) 0.5104	5.77 (L)
4.	DWR-162	TS-IR	17.00	(-) 0.9129	7.74
5.	B-Yellow	TS-RF+IR	17.95	(-) 0.7336	7.12
6.	MACS-1967	TS-RF	19.26	(-) 0.7475	6.80
7.	B-Red	TS-RF+IR	19.30	(-) 0.7519	8.31
8.	Meghdoot	TS-RF	21.57	(-) 0.5936	7.59
9.	Raj-1555	TS-IR	21.60	(-) 0.7787	6.49
10.	JU-12	TS-RF	21.80	(-) 0.8504	8.99
11.	AKW-3018	TS-RF	26.16	(-) 0.9053	6.61
12.	MACS-2496	TS-IR	26.92	(-) 0.6463	12.88
13.	MACS-9 (Akola)	TS-RF	27.10	(-) 0.9614	13.88
14.	MACS-9 (Indore)	TS-RF	27.43	(-0.8154	8.10
15.	N-59	TS-RF	31.95	(-) 0.03821 (H)	13.54
16.	Raj-911	TS-IR	32.80	(-) 0.6243	12.36
17.	A-9-30-1	TS-RF	35.40	(-) 0.1235	15.09
18.	AKW-381	TS-IR	40.92	(-) 0.1604	16.19 (H)
19.	NP-401	TS-RF+IR	43.42 (H)	(-) 0.2119	13.2
20.	Range of variation (max.-min)		28.17	1.0043	10.42

TS: timely sown; LS: late sown; (+): increase; (-): decrease; (#): information received from Senior Wheat Breeder; P, K, V, Akola Maharashtra and from Twenty-five Years of Coordinated Wheat Research (eds Tandon, J.P. and Sethi, A.P.), All India Coordinated Wheat Research Project, 1986; (L): lowest value within samples; (H): highest value within samples.

- ***Invariance of the area enclosed under normalized moisture hysteresis loop with location of growth of the variety indicative of being a genetic characteristic:***

A corollary experiment was given to one of students as his M.Sc. thesis problem. He was asked to establish normalized moisture hysteresis curves for the same varieties of wheat and species grown at four different agro-climatic locations, namely, Karnal and New Delhi in the north, Indore in the middle and Akola in the south-central peninsula during the same crop year. The most interesting observation from this thesis work being that the area enclosed within the normalized moisture hysteresis loops of individual varieties of wheat remains practically invariant within experimental limits of variation, irrespective of the location of growth of the variety. This therefore clearly indicates a genetic linkage between wheat variety and area under its normalized moisture hysteresis curve. My two detailed papers covering my studies on all the three species of wheat were immediately accepted and published in Current Science.

From the above experiment, what I had demonstrated being a definite correlation between the area enclosed by a moisture hysteresis loop of a variety and its agronomic status for cultivation under actual field conditions. In the process of this study, I had also thereby developed positively; a non-destructive, laboratory based experimental method to test and screen newly bred, breeders wheat varieties for their suitability for cultivation under rain-fed conditions before hand and before subjecting them for extensive performance and production trials at multiple locations and agro-climatic conditions. This is a huge saving on monetary expenditure involved in multi-location agronomic field trials. The method was also useful in identifying identified wheat varieties.

- ***Normalized Moisture Hysteresis Curves as Mandatory Test before Multi-location Field Trials:***

Immediately after the publication of my papers, I made a strong plea to the Director, Wheat Research, Karnal, Haryana to include area enclosed under Normalized Moisture Hysteresis Curves as a mandatory laboratory method for screening and short-listing newly bred breeder's wheat variety materials for extensive and expensive National multi-location field trials under 'All India Coordinated Wheat Improvement Project' to assess their suitability for cultivation under rain fed conditions. I sent reprint copies of my research publications justifying my pleading along with an offer to collaborate and cooperate in training some Technical Assistants in the methodology involved in such screening. I expected a very positive response and possibly some appreciation of my efforts in providing a laboratory based method for such kind of screening of wheat varieties, as there was no such auxiliary aid to the wheat breeders available in the literature. However, I was sorry to have received a reply from the Director-Wheat Research stating that –"screening for rained / drought tolerance was not their mandate".

- ***International Implications and Trans-National appreciation:***

Within a month of the publication of my papers on normalized moisture hysteresis, I started receiving requests from laboratories across the world for copies of reprints. One such request was from Dr. Luc De Bry, Head of the Research Department of M/S Danone Biscuits Nord, Herentals, Belgium. About three months later, I received a personal letter from Dr. Luc De Bry, the contents of which not only surprised me but elated me to newer heights of self confidence and sense of accomplishment to some extent. Dr. Luc De Bry had subjected my procedure to a test on wheat varieties cultivated in England, France and Turkey with a difference that he employed an automatic infrared sensor based incubator for recording his moisture hysteresis curves. Dr. Luc Bry was not only able to successfully segregate English, French and Turkish wheat varieties based on their distinct variations in hysteresis loop shapes but also screen them for characteristic property of minimum moisture absorption for use in his bakery products with enhanced shelf life. Under the European conditions, varieties that can sustain and give economic yields under excessive moisture availability as contrary to the conditions in a tropical country like India, where farmers need varieties that can sustain severe draught conditions. It is interesting to read what Dr. Luc De Bry writes about the New Concept of Normalized Moisture Hysteresis curves and the potential of the method developed as reproduced in his own words below;

Herentals. 18.11.96

Dear Dr. Moharir,

Thank you very much for the reprint of your paper "Moisture desorption and absorption isotherms for seeds of some cultivars of *Triticum dicoccum* wheat: *Curr. Sci.* 70, 1012-1017; 1996.

I thoroughly enjoyed reading it, and even re-reading it. It does not happen often that one can read papers where the author is working at cross-fertilizing the fields of plant science and physical chemistry. I do believe that your results will have profound implications in every agricultural discipline (not only in breeding), and for every crop that humans are cultivating for obtaining their foods. Up to now, I was more used to see and also to measure classical isotherms with water activity on the X-axis and moisture content on the Y-axis, and have the kinetic data separately presented. I like your presentation of "Normalized mass of seeds" over time. Your concept of hysteresis area is very talkative, very expressive. No doubt that it will prove helpful to speed up and to improve plant breeding process.

Indeed, hysteresis is appearing to be a simple and elegant mechanism for controlling gene activity. For instance, just before raining, soil and plant root cells are in a state of desorption. With the first drops of rain, they move to the state of adsorption. Once under water, root cells are in anaerobiosis, and in the absence of oxygen, glycolysis is stopped at the level of ethanol. Too high ethanol concentration is toxic for the cells, diluting cell membranes, damaging mitochondria, causing glycosol leakage etc. In order to prevent this, the gene coding for alcohol dehydrogenase is switched on. When the water stress is over, soil and plant root cells move back to the desorption isotherm, the biosynthesis of enzyme stops, and the gene is switched off. This is only one example of water activity controlling gene activity. The more we look for other examples, the more we find.

Luc De Bry, Ph.D.

Head of Research Department

(Full Text of the letter from Dr. Luc Bry is given in Figure-15)

Danone Biscuits Nord naamloze vennootschap - société anonyme

DANONE

Dr. A.V. Moharir
Nuclear Research Laboratory
Indian Agricultural Research Institute

New Dehli - 110012

INDIA

De Beukelaer - Pareinlaan 1, B-2200 Herentals, Belgium
Tel. 32-14 / 24 12 11 direct line 32-14 / 24 14 32 Telefax 32-14 /24.10.25
Email : luc.de.bry@pophost.eunet.be
h.r./r.c. turnhout 29.039 btw/tva 414.321.048

u/ref.
o/ref.

Herentals, 18.11.96

Concerns :comments and questions about your paper in Curr. Sci. 70, 1996

Dear Dr. Moharir,

Thank you very much for the reprint of your paper "Moisture desorption and absorption isotherms for seeds of some cultivars of *Triticum dicoccum* wheat; *Curr. Sci.* 70, 1012-1017; 1996.

I thoroughly enjoyed reading it, and even re-reading it. It does not happen often that one can read papers where the author is working at cross-fertilizing the fields of plant science and of physical-chemistry. I do believe that your results will have profound implications in every agricultural discipline (not only in breeding), and for every crop that humans are cultivating for obtaining their foods. Up to now, I was more used to see and also to measure classical isotherms with water activity on the X-axis and moisture content on the Y-axis, and have kinetic data separately presented. I like your presentation of "normalized mass of seeds" over time. Your concept of hystreresis area is very talkative, very expressive. No doubt that it will prove helpful to speed up and to improve plant breeding process.

Indeed, hysteresis is appearing to be a simple and elegant mechanism for controlling gene activity. For instance, just before raining, soil and plant root cells are in a state of desorption. With the first drops of rain, they move to the state of adsorption. Once under water, root cells are in anaerobiosis, and in the abscence of oxygen, glycolysis is stopped at the level of ethanol. Too high ethanol concentration is toxic for the cells, diluting cell membranes, damaging mitochondria, causing cytosol leakage, etc. In order to prevent this, the gene coding for alcohol dehydrogenase is switched on. When the water stress is over, soil and plant root cells move back to the desorption isotherm, the biosynthesis of the enzyme stops, and the gene is switched off. This is only one exemple of water activity controlling gene activity. The more we look for other examples, the more we find.

As your paper is more centered on wheat varieties in plant breeding than on seed thermodynamics, I wonder if you are familiar with the work of one of the best physical chemist that I know, i.e. Prof. T.P. Labuza, Vice-Dean of the University of Minnesota, at Minneapolis, USA. He has worked an awful lot on isotherms, water activity or chemical potential of the water, microbiology, reaction kinetics and the thermodynamics underlying all isotherms. He is very good at maths, highly skilled with the use of all isotherm equations and is recognized as a world leader in his field. If not, I shall be happy to send you a copy of some of his most cited papers. I may be wrong in my assumption, but I am sure that you will like it, write to him, and manage to meet him at some relevant congress.

What you said (on page 1013) about isotherms of rainfed *vs* irrigated varieties of *T. aestivum* and *T. durum* is intriguing me. Therefore, would you please be so kind and send me a copy of your relevant publications, Moharir A.V. (1994) and Moharir A.V. & Rakash N. (1995) ? - Should you happen to visit Belgium or Netherlands, I would happy to discuss about our respective wheat and water stress researches and further complement them. For instance, by contrast to India, our Lowland Countries are rather over-rainfed, and irrigated to get the water out of the land and to the sea.

While looking forward to hearing from you and to reading your other papers, I want to thank you again for the first reprint that you so kindly sent to me.

With anticipated thanks and kind regards,

Luc De Bry

Luc De Bry, Ph.D.
Head of Research Department

Figure 15; Full text of the letter received from Dr. Luc De Bry

Dr. Luc Bry later invited me to Herentals, Belgium for three days to discuss the possibility of submitting a joint collaborative research project with financial support from the Commission of European Communities, Brussels, Belgium, during my visit to Ghent Belgium on a senior Fellowship from the Commission of European Communities in 1997-1998. I also delivered a seminar on my studies on Normalized Moisture Hysteresis Curves and screening wheat genotypes for rain-fed cultivation on the basis of the area enclosed under the hysteresis curves at the Danone Biscuits in Herentals. The seminar was not only attended by all the research personnel from the affiliated companies of Danone Biscuits from all the European countries but also by Dr. David Jessa, who flew in especially for the seminar from the USA.

Despite all this and at least five more papers published by other fellow scientists on Normalized moisture hysteresis in relation to draught tolerance, this innovative contribution has continued to be overlooked by the institute / ICAR authorities and even by the plant breeders for further exploration. In realty, the breeders should have felt excited because, this method would have saved considerable time and effort in conducting field trials for the newly bred varieties.

In an attempt to establish Normalized Moisture Hysteresis and its role in screening for draught tolerance on solid scientific foundation, within the stipulated time frame of two to three years, I submitted my proposal for a project under the scheme of Emeritus Scientist after superannuating in 2006, but alas, only to be turned down with most unscientific and illogical comment received from only one reviewer of the project proposal and without being given a chance to present it before a duly constituted committee of experts. This is how support to science and scientific research is generally decided in this country and this must change at the earliest. Only a science administrator with some original personal contribution to science to his credit, competence to hybridize ideas from different disciplines, open and magnanimous mind, and sincere convictions in science and technology as a vehicle of change in the quality of life of the masses can bring about a significant improvement in administration of science.

32

Contribution in Structure-Property Relation Studies in Native Cotton Fibres

• A Chance encounter that changed the course of my life

In the year 1975, Professor J. Sikorsky from the University of Leeds, England delivered a series of lectures on Electron Microscopic study of Textile Fibres at the Textile Technology Department of the Indian Institute of Technology in Delhi. The organizers sent out circular and invitations to all scientists working in Electron Microscopy laboratories in various organizations in Delhi for attending these seminars. As a new entrant in the science of electron microscopy and eager to equip myself with ability to handle all kind of specimens for their microscopic observation, I immediately sought permission from the Project Director-NRL to attend lectures of Professor J. Sikorski. Dr. B. C. Panda from the Division of Agricultural Physics, who had previous experience of working on Small Angle X-Ray diffraction study on sheep-wool fibres for his Ph.D., degree was also interested and we both decided to go together for a week for the seminars.

Professor Sikorski was not unknown to me because I had read a good number of his papers on applications of electron microscopy to textile fibres published in the Journal of Microscopy of the Royal Microscopical Society of England. It was during this lecture series, both I and Dr. B. C. Panda got introduced to Dr. Vidya Bhushan (V. B.) Gupta **(Fig.3)**, a renowned polymer physicist and Professor in the host Department of Textile Technology, Indian Institute of Technology, New Delhi. Dr. V. B. Gupta was very keen to diversify from synthetic fibres and initiate some work on natural fibres such as wool, jute, flax or cotton. Having come to know that Dr. Panda was a Senior Physicist working in the Indian Agricultural Research Institute in New Delhi itself and where cotton breeding and cotton growing was a regular ongoing activity, Dr. V. B. Gupta proposed a collaborative project to Dr. B. C. Panda with a request to find some student who can be given registration to pursue his Ph.D. degree under their collective guidance in the collaborative project. Almost instantaneously, Dr. B. C. Panda introduced me to Dr. V. B. Gupta as a potential student who can be given registration as I fulfilled almost all the requirements that Dr. Gupta was asking for? Immediately on return back to IARI, I moved my papers for permission to initiate a collaborative project with IIT-Delhi from the Director-IARI. The weird rules of the institute did not promise a smooth passage for me. I had to lodge several representations against the existing rules and point out how detrimental they were to the career prospects of young scientists. Fortunately, Dr. Kissen Kanungo, Dean and Joint Director Education and Dr. A. B. Joshi, Director-IARI saw reason and merit in my representation. They systematically got the rules suitably amended through the institute Academic and Research Councils respectively and I was granted permission to start my collaboration with IIT-Delhi in the month of October 1975. However, Indian Institute of Technology (Delhi) in their turn, granted me registration with retrospective effect from January 1975, thereby saving almost a year for my research. I submitted my Ph.D. thesis in 1979 and pleasantly received my degree in the 1980 convocation of IIT-Delhi. This convocation was addressed by none other than my own boss Professor M. S. Swaminathan FRS, Director General of the Indian Council of Agricultural Research, as the chief guest.

- **On the course to defining suitable problem for collaborative project**

My immediate priority now was to identify and define a definitive problem for the collaborative research project and my Ph.D. theses. Whatever problem I identified, it had to be justified within the research and priority mandates of both the IARI and the IIT-Delhi. Extensive reading of recent research reviews, scanning through the abstracting journals and discussions with cotton breeders of the institute indicated that breeders actually did not have a reliable parameter for screening parent genotypes for use in their hybridization program of breeding new varieties with inherent high fibre tenacity. The prevalent fibre testing and characterization methods were subjective, sensitive to environmental conditions and grossly unreliable. Cotton breeders therefore need a reliable parameter for screening parent genotypes for producing hybrids with improved fibre tenacity because tenacity of fibres is known to be genetically inherited parameter in cotton.

Another emerging scenario in the early seventies was the development of the Rotor/Open End Spinning Technology (OES) and fast replacement of the Ring Frame Spinning frames with rotor spinning spindles in textile industry. OES being seven times faster in drawing yarns than Ring Frame System, demands increased fibre tenacity, fineness and staple length as the primary requisites on raw cotton fibre properties in order of preference. This essentially is opposite to the requirement of fibre staple length, fineness and fibre tenacity by the ring frame system. Moreover, almost 90% of yarn production in the seventies was in the 30s' counts in view of the fact that almost all the cotton lint production in India was of the category of short and medium staple type. Open End Spinning was therefore believed to had a very bright future, but called for immediate change in our cotton breeding priority of breeding for increased staple length to breeding for increased fibre tenacity. Providing cotton breeders with a reliable parameter for tensile strength of fibres and research for such a parameter was therefore a foremost priority.

- **Preparing Blue-Print and adopting strategy for the Research Project**

It was therefore decided to take a fresh look at all the important physical, chemical, structural and technological properties of cotton fibres using all sophisticated instrumental facilities at our disposal such as polarized and light optical microscopes, Transmission and Scanning electron microscopes, X-Ray diffraction besides modern and conventional instrumental testing equipments. The most important decision that we took in defining our problem for research being to confine our studies to a large number of varieties released for commercial cultivation of only one species of cotton and a few F1 hybrids amongst themselves. Moreover, all these varieties and their hybrids must have been grown at one location, one farm and in the same year of cotton growing season. This was essential to subtract the influence of climate, season, location and cultivation practices on cotton fibre properties and for comparison of properties amongst varieties grown under identical agronomic production conditions. This was essential to compare and contrast purely the contribution of genetics in determining the fibre quality and properties, a point that was observed to have been missed by workers in studies reported earlier in the literature. In view of this decision, I feel that the results arrived at from my research work (and later extended to varieties of all the four commercial species of cotton) are unique, comprehensive and far more reliable than similar studies previously reported in the literature but without taking any notice of the environmental conditions, location of growth, species of cotton and agronomic production conditions under which the fibres reported on, were grown into consideration. Much of the conflicting reports on structure-property relationships of cotton fibres in the literature are as I feel, due to this neglect in selecting fibre samples studied.

- **Selection of Cotton Varieties and supply of Fibres for IARI-IIT-Delhi collaborative Project Study**

It just happened that during the period, I was busy in defining my research project in meticulous details; Dr. Chandrakant T. (C. T.) Patel, the celebrated cotton breeder from Surat Gujrat, who gave India a lead in commercial production of hybrid cotton for the first time in the world *(with his H-4, commercial hybrid variety)* was visiting IARI. I lost no opportunity to meet him during his leisure time and take his advice on my proposed research project. Fortunately for me, it was Dr. Patel, in consultation with Dr. J. E. Siddique, Senior Cotton Breeder from IARI, not only identified the varieties of *Gossypium hirsutum* species for my study from breeder variety collection at Surat in Gujrat but also promised to provide adequate amount of ginned fibres for my comprehensive study including mechanical testing.

The same criteria was followed by me in the selection of varieties of the other three species of cotton namely *Gossypium arboretum, Gossypium herbaceum and Gossypium barbadense* in my attempt to extend my work in subsequent years beyond 1980 as a life-time mission to all the four commercial species of cotton cultivated primarily for lint fibres. A large number of same cotton varieties of individual four species were grown at four different agro-climatic locations namely; New Delhi and Sirsa in the north, Nagpur in central India and Coimbatore in the south, on same farm at each location and in the same crop year under uniform agronomic production conditions so as to assess purely genetic differences in fibre properties of individual varieties and species cultivated and grown under identical environmental and agronomic production conditions from each location and environmental fluctuations in fibre properties of individual variety arising between locations. This extensive work and perhaps only of its kind done nowhere else in the world was carried out under a collaborative research project between the IARI and State University of Ghent in Belgium with financial assistance from the European Economic Communities for four years from 1994-1998. In these attempts, I received excellent support and cooperation from Dr. Munshi Singh and Dr. V. P. Singh, Senior Cotton Breeders from IARI and Breeders from Central Institute for Cotton Research at Nagpur, Sirsa and Coimbatore. Ginned fibres of all the same varieties of individual species of *Gossypium hirsutum*, *Gossypium barbadense Gossypium arboretum* and *Gossypium herbaceum* grown at the four locations were collected for research and analysis. Besides, I received award of a Senior Fellowship from the Commission of European Communities, 1990-91 and Project Financial Support from the National Technology Mission on Cotton launched by the Government of India that sustained my research work in this area of research on cotton.

- **Strategy adopted for characterization of fibres for individual characteristics and importance of the right kind of samples for study**

The most obvious strategy I adopted for characterization of fibres for individual properties being to first compile an up to date review of the literature on individual fibre property of cotton and then decide about the most appropriate method, instrument, sample preparation, sample size, statistical analysis, comparative evaluation etc. With this, I not only prepared myself to write comprehensive review articles on most of the fibre property parameters but could also take an objective look on each of these properties from the point of view of my own results on fibres grown under uniform conditions from individual species and locations. All this also helped me to demonstrate how observations and results on my set of samples were more representative of the inherent genetic differences between varieties and species and not influenced by the environmental conditions of growth. This would be illustrated further at appropriate places. Out of 37 years of my service at the IARI, I spent nearly 30 years in doing research on structure and structure-property studies on native cotton fibres and produced results of rare quality and purity that I feel very strongly, had never been done in the past because of the fact that very selection of the cotton fibre material for such reported investigations was faulty. Results described here in the following pages are a consolidated summary of the work done on cotton fibres.

- **Current understanding on the Structure of the native Cotton fibre and their morphological characterization**

Cotton fibres are not fibres in textile sense but elongated cylindrical single cells from the epidermis of cotton seeds. Fibre formation begins on the day of flowering and pollination. Cotton fibre development takes place within cotton bolls in three distinct phases generally described as (i) elongation period (ii) secondary maturation period and (iii) dehydration period. During the elongation period, tubular fibre cells simply elongate to their maximum lengths and consist only of primary wall of cellulose fibrils filled with cytoplasmic fluid inside. The elongation continues for fifteen to 25 days depending upon species and environmental conditions of growth at the location. At the end of elongation period, the secondary maturation period begins, during which, coaxial diurnal secondary layers of pure crystalline cellulose are deposited inside along the primary walls. Secondary layer deposition continues for thirty to seventy days depending upon the species and environmental conditions at the location of growth of cotton. Electron microscopic evidence however suggests that both elongation and secondary deposition proceed concurrently. At the end of the secondary maturation, the cotton bolls within which fibre development takes place, are cut off from the transpiration stream of plants and the contents of cotton bolls begin to dehydrate. The elongated cylindrical fibre cells collapse into flat convoluted ribbons as the dehydration proceeds. Careful observations made by me suggest that process of formation of convolution twists begins close to the tip of the fibres and proceed towards the base as dehydration period advances. Fluffy white dehydrated seed-cotton fibres are picked up manually or with the help of harvesting machines. Machine harvested seed cotton generally pick-up trash and leaf material along with cotton as compared to hand-picked cotton. The farmer is always put to economic loss depending upon the amount of trash content in his produce because the textile mills have to spend extra energy in cleaning lint cotton for removal of trash before processing. It was my observation that just cracked cotton bolls from the field when subjected to dehydration at 30-35^0 C in an oven, become as fluffy as in the field dried condition. Very clean, trash free cotton can thus be harvested by picking just cracked bolls and dehydrating them in drying cabinets. The technology for harvesting clean trash-free cotton was demonstrated effectively but could not be pursued to work out the entire economics and commercial viability. Harvested seed cotton is then subjected to ginning for mechanical separation of fibres from the seeds. The separated loose fluffy ginned fibres called the lint-cotton are compacted into bales of 180 kg each under hydraulic press for easy transportation and trade and become the starting raw material in textile industry for spinning yarns and finally weaving them into cloth. Chemically, cotton fibres constitute 97% pure cellulose, a naturally synthesized biopolymer, diurnally deposited in coaxially laid secondary layers along the primary wall inside the cell matrix. A polymer consists of a chain of similar molecules joined end to end and forming a long linear strand. The number of molecular units joined together is described as the degree of polymerization, which may be in thousands. Cellulose polymer in cotton is diurnally deposited in coaxially secondary layers along the primary wall inside the cell matrix. Whereas the cellulose of the primary wall consists of cross oriented cellulose micro-fibrils, the cellulose of the diurnally laid secondary walls consists of left- oriented spirals of cellulose micro-fibrils. The angular orientation of these left-oriented spirals increases towards the fibre axis as the secondary deposition proceeds. The average numbers of secondary layers during fibre-maturation / cotton boll maturation period varies from about 30 in diploid to as many as 70 or more in tetraploid species **(Figure 15)**. So also, the number of reversal extinction bands observed under crossed polarized light, per unit length of fibres is more in tetraploid species as compared to that in the diploid species of cotton. The number of convoluted twists (Convolutions) along the length of dehydrated fibre ribbons has long been disputed to be genetic and environmental in their origin and there was no unanimity on this view until my comprehensive research conducted on cotton varieties of the same varieties and species, cultivated at four different agro-climatic location in the same crop growing year finally proved that convolutions are genetic in their origin ***(Reference 18).*** The thick, short-staple fibres of diploid *Gossypium arboretum* and *Gossypium herbaceum* species have fewer convolutions on them as compared to the medium and long staple fibres of the tetraploid *Gossypium hirsutum* and *Gossypium barbadense* species. Convolution twists enable cotton fibres to be spun into yarns by providing inter-fibre grip and preventing slippage of fibres in yarns but are also known to affect orientation of crystalline cellulose micro-fibrils along fibre length and X-ray crystallite orientation angles. Subtraction of average convolution angle from average value of X-Ray orientation angle for a variety is believed to provide value of the true spiral angle in un-convoluted / never-dried fibre. Several workers believed that true spiral angle irrespective of species and variety is constant and several others believed that true spiral angle in cotton need not be constant and varies between varieties and species of cotton. It was again the comprehensive research done by me ***(Reference 18-26)*** that finally set to rest the controversy over constancy of true spiral angle to show that its values vary within varieties and species of cotton although the range of variation is very narrow. The average X-Ray orientation angle was not only identified to be the best index for characterization of fibres for their tenacity but genetically invariant for individual varieties when grown at different agro-climatic locations. Also, in the first ever research report published of its kind, my research clearly demonstrated that the average size of cellulose crystallites synthesized and deposited within developing cotton fibres, irrespective of species, variety and location of their growth remains practically invariant ***(Reference 19).*** Experimental microscopic observations on developing cotton fibres under crossed polarized light indicated that the first dark reversal extinction band was observed in a 16 days old fibre from flowering date and frequency of bands increased with each day of maturity with reduction in inter-band spacing. Reversal frequency within and between varieties and species of cotton has also been a subject of intensive debate besides controversy of their being genetic or environmental in origin. Exhaustive work conducted by me in this respect finally proved that 'Reversals' and their frequency are indeed genetic and vary within and between varieties of species. Several researchers had tried to establish coincidental correlation between location of reversal band along fibre length under crossed polarized light and external convolution twists on fibres. It was again left to me to demonstrate that such coincidence was purely restricted to the plane of observation of fibres under microscope field and when the plane of observation changed, the coincidence was no longer seen. There is therefore no structural coincidence between reversals and convolution twists ***(Reference 20).***

Much of the work on convolutions and reversals I pursued and extended further was based on the work done earlier by the group of scientists headed by Professor Gilbert E. Raes in Belgium. Incidentally, Professor Raes, as the Director of the Laboratorium De Muelemeester Voor Technologie der Textielstoffen, was a member of the International Committee of Technical and Scientific Experts, who had gone into establishing the authenticity of the coffin cloth known as the 'Turin Shroud' which bears the facial and body impression resembling like figure of Jesus Christ. It just happened that while on a fellowship from the Commission of the European Communities in 1990-91 at the State University of Ghent-Belgium, I sought opportunity to meet Professor Raes who had since retired long ago but had settled in Ghent itself. Having come to Belgium, I would not have been able to excuse myself if I had returned back to India without meeting Professor Gilbert Raes and therefore requested the Secretary in the Department to provide me his contact telephone number. Following week, I contacted Professor Raes and introduced myself and explained my eagerness to meet him more as a courtesy as I had progressed in my work on convolutions and reversals in cotton from where he had left. "where, do you want me to come and meet you? He asked". No Sir, you need not bother, I would come to meet you wherever you ask me to do so, I said. "OK, you can come to my residence at 9.00 AM sharp tomorrow morning but remember that I will give you only fifteen minutes" said Professor Raes. Next day morning, I reached his doorstep fifteen minutes earlier and exactly at 9.00 AM rang his door bell **(Figure 16 a)**.

Figure 16 a: Dr. A. V. Moharir (Left) with Professor Gilbert E. Raes in Ghent-Belgium

Figure 16 b; Dr. A. V. Moharir (Left) with Professor T. Fransen in Ghent-Belgium

Come in gentleman and quickly, without wasting much time in formalities I engaged myself into explaining my own work on morphological structure of cotton fibres and my interpretations. This dialogue continued for well over three hours without each one of us noticing how time flew past. Neither Professor Raes indicated that the time limit, he had given for my visit that was already over since long nor did I realize so in my eagerness and enthusiasm to explain my work. At the end, Professor Raes said, "Moharir, I am not satisfied and I wish to meet you again for more discussion". And immediately next week following our first meeting, I received invitation from Professor Raes for lunch in one of the decent restaurants in Ghent. He also invited Professor T. Fransen and Professor L. Vershraege, his colleagues and co-authors on most of his publications to join both of us. Not only this, Professor Raes gave me lift in his car after the lunch and dropped me at my laboratory gate before saying goodbye **(Figure 16 a).** Meeting with Professor Gilbert Raes was memorable for me as I got the first hand information about the 'Turin Shroud' from himself and the way he had analyzed the piece of shroud cloth. The corner from where he took his sample from the 'Turin Shroud' is today known as the 'Raes Corner'. Microscopic examination of some of the threads from the shroud done by Professor Raes indicated a 'herringbone weave' which in ancient times was found only in costly materials. Traces of cotton mixed in the weave were also noticed which suggested that the shroud was probably woven on a loom meant for weaving cotton cloth. Moreover the cotton fibres he had identified were of the type grown only in the Middle East and it was not available in Europe until 800 AD.

The fact that cotton fibres consist of almost 97% pure cellulose, much of the research on cotton was also directed to determining the fine structure of cellulose, crystal structure, crystal lattice, lattice spacing and width of cellulose elementary fibrils, as assembled in nature using X-Ray diffraction, Transmission and Scanning Electron Microscopes and such other physical techniques. Early reports showed variations in widths of cellulose micro fibrils between varieties of different species and there was no unanimity over the actual width of fibrils although micro-fibrils of about 3.5 nm were commonly seen. However, it was again my research that showed for the first time, cellulose elementary fibrils of 2.0 nm width resolved under transmission electron microscope (Philips EM-300) from negatively stained ultrasonically disintegrated cotton fibres ***(Reference 20, 21)***. These elementary fibrils are stacked parallel to make bundles of microfibrils.

• X-Ray Diffraction Studies on Cotton Fibres

It is now well established that technological performance of cotton depends on the fine structure of fibres. Transmission (TEM) and Scanning (SEM) electron microscopes and their other variants, the Nuclear Magnetic Resonance (NMR) and X-Ray diffraction techniques provide means to study the fine structure of matter at levels of molecular resolution, and have been successfully applied to elucidate fine structure of cotton fibres. Modern developments in cotton processing technologies are demanding a major shift in cotton breeding priority from breeding cotton for increased staple length to increased inherent tensile strength of fibres. Moreover, strength of cotton fibers is not only known to be heritable but environmentally the most stable of many fibre properties in view of the fact that cotton crop is known to highly location specific. The modern Open-End-Spinning technology (OES), which is about seven times more faster in spinning yarns over the conventional Ring-Frame-Spinning, is demanding tensile strength as the first requisite on raw fibre properties over fineness and staple length. The Ring-Frame Spinning required staple length over fineness and tensile strength in order of importance, as the first requisite on fibre properties. No wonder, all attempts in the last six decades were directed in increasing the staple length of the indigenous cotton varieties for production of super-fine quality textiles. However, cotton breeders, so far had no reliable method of choosing parent genetic root stock in hybridization for transferring and increasing tensile strength of fibres of hybrid varieties evolved and they often had to resort to hit and trial strategies. The procedure is not only laborious and time consuming but economically expensive besides uncertainty in realization of desired results for reasons beyond human control. The existing methods for measurement of tensile strength of fibres were known to be grossly subjective. Therefore, in an attempt to help the cotton breeders for screening the right parent cotton genotypes for their hybridization for increased strength of fibers and extent of location specificity, it was decided to take a fresh unbiased look at all the important physical and technological properties of fibres and ultra-structure besides rates of cellulose synthesis and deposition within fibres, at various developing stages and at full maturity, using sophisticated and diverse instrumental techniques, such as optical and polarized light optical microscopes, transmission and scanning electron microscopes and X-ray diffraction, besides conventional and modern methods of testing fibres for morphological and technological properties. I am happy that most of these ventures and bold initiative produced unexpectedly newer findings which revised some of the older prevalent concepts about structural features of cotton fibre proposed way back in 1932 AD by W. L. Balls. Application of Transmission and scanning electron microscopy for studies of cotton fibres was not new, yet they provided considerable scope for further understanding. The limitations being that no developing live cotton fibres could be successively studied for several days by these techniques. The Negative staining technique using transmission electron microscope on ultrasonically disintegrated developing cotton fibres at various maturity stages obtained from green unopened cotton bolls showed that the finest cellulose elementary fibrils of 2.0 nm width, irrespective of the species of cotton, could be resolved with a high resolution transmission electron microscope (Philips EM-300) as against the 3.5 nm wide cellulose fibrils commonly seen and reported. This observation later found support from several other workers in the field ***(Reference – 20, 21)***.

Cotton fibres consist of about 97% pure cellulose and this cellulose is almost 100% crystalline in nature. Cotton Fibres singly or in well parallelized bundles produce characteristic X-Ray diffraction patterns which tell about the spirally oriented disposition of cellulose in the form of long bundles of micro-fibrils, deposited in coaxial diurnal secondary layers inside the elongated epidermal seed hairs called the cotton fibres. A well matured cotton fibre consists of 35 to 75 individual coaxial telescoping secondary layers, within ~ 20 micron wide elongated epidermal cellular cells / fibres, depending upon the species and environmental conditions at the location of growth of cotton **(Fig. 17)**.

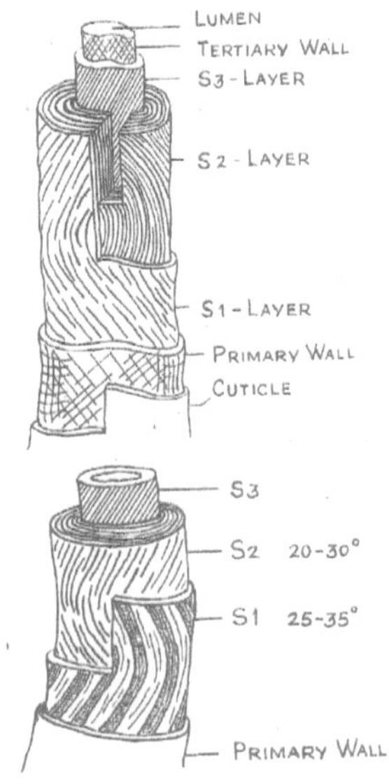

Figure 17: Schematic diagram of the spiral structure of cotton fibre

With longer fibre length and extended secondary deposition period (corresponding to cotton boll maturation period) there is increased orientation of crystalline cellulose micro-fibrils to the cotton fibre axis. Such increased orientation leads to increased inherent tensile strength of fibres, a desired fibre property for the new processing technology. Therefore, from the X-ray diffraction studies on bundles of well parallelized cotton fibres, the weighted average value of orientation of cellulose crystallites along fibre axis known as the Herman's orientation factor was identified to be significantly better correlated with both single fibre and bundle fibre tenacities than the conventionally used 40, 50 or 75% X-ray angles evaluated as the angles to fibre axis where X-ray intensity along the equatorial [002] diffraction arcs drop down to 40, 50 or 75 % of the incident intensity. And both, within varieties of individual species, within a mixture of varieties of two tetraploid and two diploid species and within a mixture of varieties of all the four species of cotton taken together, the Herman's orientation factor was observed to retain its superiority over the 40, 50 and 75% X-ray angles in correlating with fibre tenacity **(Table-2)**. It has therefore been emphatically proposed that selection of cotton genotypes for hybridization for increased strength of fibres must necessarily be done on the basis of the values of their Herman's orientation factor. Higher values of Herman's factor corresponding to increased value of inherent tenacity of fibres ***(Reference19).***

Detailed X-Ray diffraction studies on fine structure of fibres of the same cotton varieties grown at four agro-climatically different geographic locations in the country have revealed that whereas the values of fine structural parameters such as 40, 50 and 75% X-ray angles (Figure-2), change with location of growth of varieties, the Herman's crystallite orientation factors, average cellulose crystallite sizes, frequency of convolution twists and reversal extinction bands (observed under crossed polarized light) along length of fibres, within individual varieties, remain practically invariant with change of location of growth of cotton. The rates of cellulose synthesis and consequently the maturity of fibres however, vary with location of growth of cotton. These important findings, reported for the first time in the literature from studies from a well-planned comprehensive study on fibres of a large number of varieties of all the four individual commercial species of cotton, grown species-wise under identical agro-climatic conditions can be of great practical significance in cotton breeding for not only identifying location specific varieties but for unraveling the fundamental basic inter-relationships between various fibre physical and technological properties with their fine-structural characteristics, using carefully selected and specially grown varieties of the four species subtracting environmental influences for effective comparison and evaluation, never before attempted as such in the history of cotton research.

Such attempt and kind of growing cotton varieties and generation of fibre samples for comparative evaluation of fine structure of fibres of different varieties and species had been done for the first time in the entire history of cotton research.

Table 2: Correlations of Hermans factor and other X-ray orientation parameters with bundle fibre tenacity within individual species and between mixture of varieties of diploid and tetraploid species of cotton

Sl. No.	Cotton species	40% x-ray angle	50% x-ray angle	75% x-ray angle	$\square_m$	Hermans factor f
1.	*G. hirsutum*	$r = -0.413$ $p > 0.05$	$r = -0.442$ $p > 0.05$	$r = -0.476$ $p > 0.02$	$r = -0.727$ $p > 0.001$	$r = 0.712$ $p > 0.001$
2.	*G. barbadense*	$r = -0.582$ $p > 0.005$	$r = -0.536$ $p > 0.01$	$r = -0.131$ p (insignificant)	$r = -0.797$ $p > 0.001$	$r = 0.745$ $p > 0.001$
3.	*G. arboreum*	$r = -0.830$ $p > 0.001$	$r = -0.785$ $p > 0.001$	$r = -0.618$ $p > 0.001$	$r = -0.824$ $p > 0.001$	$r = 0.824$ $p > 0.001$
4.	*G. harbaceum*	$r = -0.778$ $p > 0.001$	$r = -0.763$ $p > 0.001$	$r = -0.754$ $p > 0.001$	$r = -0.778$ $p > 0.001$	$r = 0.764$ $p > 0.001$
5.	New world cottons taken together *G. hirsutum* + *G. barbadense*	$r = -0.218$ $p > 0.1$	$r = -0.206$ $p > 0.1$	$r = -0.170$ $p > 0.25$	$r = -0.516$ $p > 0.0005$	$r = 0.504$ $p > 0.0005$
6.	Old-world cotton taken together *G. arboreum* + *G. harbaceum*	$r = -0.524$ $p > 0.0005$	$r = -0.369$ $p > 0.005$	$r = -0.132$ $p > 0.25$	$r = -0.768$ $p > 0.0005$	$r = 0.762$ $p > 0.0005$
7.	New- and Old-world cottons taken together *G. hirsutum* + *G. barbadense* + *G. arboreum* + *G. harbaceum*	$r = -0.253$ $p > 0.01$	$r = -0.130$ $p > 0.1$	$r = -0.005$ p (insignificant)	$r = -0.687$ $p > 0.0005$	$r = 0.694$ $p > 0.0005$

- **Revelation of Inter-Species Genetic Linkages**

An unpublished corollary analyzed from the values of Herman's Orientation Factor of large number of varieties of individual commercial species of cotton, in which varieties within each species were numbered and arranged sequentially in increasing value of their Herman's Orientation Factors, **Table 3**. These varieties are identified, species wise as per their serial numbers given in the **Table-3,** and corresponding number interval along X-axis chosen arbitrarily at convenient distance for clarity in **(Fig. 17).**

Table 3: Variation of the values of Hermans Orientation Factor within varieties of individual species of cotton studied

Sr. No.	*Gossypium arbadense*	Hermans Factor	*Gossypium hirsutum*	Hermans Factor	*Gossypium herbaceum*	Hermans Factor	*Gossypium arboreum*	Hermans Factor
	Tetraploid Name of variety (*)		**Tetraploid Name of variety (**)**		**Diploid Name of variety (***)**		**Diploid Name of variety (#)**	
1	SB-289 E	0.531	Am.Nectariless X SV-13	0.568	BD-8	0.558	G-27 X 1946	0.416
2	G-112-A-A-45	0.535	D-33	0.576	1027 ALF	0.580	Daulat	0.417
3	EC-98252	0.565	Acala 4-42	0.591	5510	0.586	Shyamli	0.432
4	17 / 3	0.591	B-1007	0.592	Kalyan	0.596	G-27 X CJ-73	0.435
5	EC-97618	0.594	Reba B50 X C120	0.597	5497	0.597	G-27 X Daulat	0.438
6	IBSI-53	0.596	H-14	0.598	V- 796	0.601	Shyamli X Virnar	0.439
7	Menoufi	0.600	LH-299	0.604	Vijay	0.619	Shyamli X 905	0.448
8	EC-97623	0.609	K-2421	0.607	4208 / 838	0.628	G-27 X 975	0.451
9	EC-97619	0.610	SV-13XAm. Nectariless	0.618	5495	0.629	905	0.466
10	GIZA-12	0.623	C120	0.621	G Cot 13 (53-3-1)	0.630	Shyamli X Daulat	0.467
11	EC-97625	0.654	Bikaneri Narma	0.628	4011	0.633	Shyamli X Y-1	0.482
12	EC-97639	0.664	C120 X B-1007	0.628	10746	0.636	G-27 X AKH-4	0.496
13	GIZA-1461	0.664	Lankart-57	0.637	Suyog	0.643	Y-1	0.496
14	CBS-34	0.668	Am. Nectariless	0.640	4042	0.647	Shyamli X 877	0.513
15	EC-104729	0.673	K-2421 X SV-213	0.647	Vijalpa	0.653	Shyamli X AKH-4	0.515
16	EC-97631	0.676	Acala 4-42 X Lankart-57	0.663	7502	0.664	G-27 X 905	0.531
17	EC-97638	0.676	B-1007 X Lankart-57	0.664	Digvijay	0.664	Virnar	0.534
18	EC-97630	0.677	D-40	0.670	G Cot 10 (1440)	0.665	AKH-4	0.537
19	EC-97634	0.683	Reba B-50	0.711	3518	0.666	G-27	0.555
20	EC-4530	0.689	—	—	4283	0.669	Shyamli X 875	0.585
21	EC-101786	0.697	—	—	3604	0.673	Shyamli X 1946	0.595
22	42 /5-W	0.712	—	—	6437	0.687	G-27 X 877	0.639
23	CBS- 148	0.741	—	—	10941	0.689	CJ-73	0.671
24	Sujata	0.743	—	—	6455	0.696	—	—
25	Suvin	0.796	—	—	5004	0.699	—	—

(*) Grown at Coimbatore 1983; (**) Grown at New Delhi 1975; (***) Grown at Surat 1983; (#) Grown at Sirsa 1978

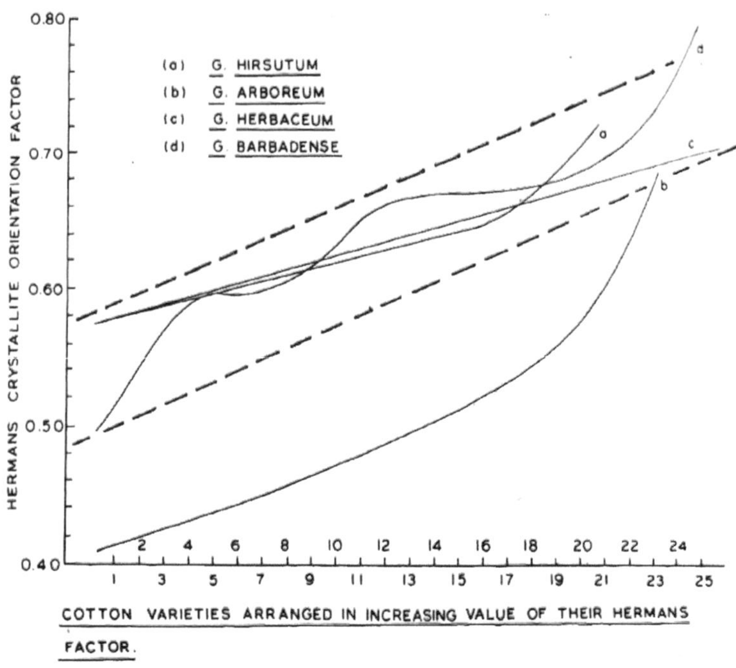

Figure 17: Variations of Herman's factor values in varieties of four species of cotton marked in their increasing order of values

The factual experimental values of Herman's Orientation Factors of individual varieties were marked corresponding to their serial number along the Y-axis. Honestly speaking, although this does not represent a correlative graph between two variables about cotton varieties but a graphical representation of the trend and range of variations of values of Herman's Factor, from the lowest to the highest values, within sample genotypes of individual species **(Fig. 17).** It would be interesting to note that the trend-curve line joining the individual value points of Herman's Factor for varieties of tetraploid *Gossypium barbadense* species lies at the top indicating that varieties of this species have higher values for Herman's factor and fibres of these varieties are not only highly oriented in respect of cellulose fibrillar orientation but also in tensile strength. Such trend-curves within varieties of tetraploid *Gossypium hirsutum* and diploid *Gossypium herbaceum* and *Gossypium arboretum* species follow immediately below the trend-curve for *Gossypium barbadense* in the sequential order. The interesting point to be marked from the trend-curves for individual species being; that the trend-curve for varieties of diploid *Gossypium arboretum* species lies too far below the trend-curves for the other three species. The trend-curves for the tetraploid *Gossypium barbadense* and *Gossypium hirsutum* species are understandably very close to each other.

Surprisingly, the trend-curve for the diploid *Gossypium herbaceum* species also lays close to the two tetraploid species referred above than to be close to the diploid *Gossypium arboretum* species. This analysis beautifully brings out the relationships between the four commercial species of cotton. The reasons for such close correspondence of values of Herman's Orientation factor within *Gossypium herbaceum* species with those of the varieties of the tetraploid *Gossypium barbadense* and *Gossypium hirsutum* can be possibly seen from the evolutionary genetic history of the tetraploid species of cotton and the fact that *Gossypium herbaceum* is the progenitor of all the tetraploid species of cotton in the world. This historical message is beautifully conveyed and reflected from the above analysis with a conviction that the Herman's orientation factor (X-Ray Crystallite Orientation Index) is certainly a genetic characteristic of cotton fibres and species and tensile strength of fibres. This is the reason, why screening of parent genetic varieties of cotton in breeding new varieties for increased tensile strength of fibres has been emphatically recommended to be done for use by the cotton breeders. And these results follow from study of a large number of cotton varieties exclusively grown species wise at the same location, same farm and in same crop growing season, subtracting thereby the environmental influence for effective comparison between varieties and fibre characteristics ***(References 19-26)***. Much of the confusion in research on structure-property correlation studies on cotton published prior to 1980 arose from the fact that researchers neglected or did not bother about the environmental conditions under which their sample fibre cotton was grown. This was important for a very highly location-specific crop such as cotton. And therefore this is the most important consideration that adds value, reliability and credibility to my research on structure-property relationship in native cotton as a strong theoretical base for breeding new varieties with inherently high tensile strength of fibres, using Herman's crystallite orientation factor values for selection of parent genotypes for hybridization.

The fresh and innovative approach I had adopted in looking at all the important morphological, physical and structural properties of cotton fibres, brought me in close personal knowledge and acquaintance of some renowned cotton researchers in the country and they included, Dr. A. B. Joshi, Dr. C. T. Patel, Dr. V. Sundaram, Dr. S. M. Betrabet, Dr. N. B. Patil, Dr. V. G. Munshi, Dr. K. R. Krishna Iyer, Dr. P. A. Chidambareshwaram, Dr. K. M. Paralikar, Dr. N. E. Dweltz, Dr. R. P. Nachane, Dr. A. K. Basu, Dr. J. E. Siddiqui, Dr. Munshi Singh, and several others and internationally in close corresponding contacts with Dr. R. St. J. Manley, Dr. K. E. Duckett, Dr. Barbara Triplett, Dr. Lloyd B. De Luca, Sir R. D. Preston (FRS), DR. H. Mark, Professor Gilbert E. Raes, Dr. L. Vershraege, Dr. T. Fransen, Professor L. Waterkeyn, Dr. Ms. Christine Peeters, Professor Paul Kiekens and many others. It was my honour to have exchanged personal correspondence with them and physically met most of these giants and receive valuable suggestions, encouragement, critical comments and even appreciation on whatever I could contribute on structure-property correlation studies on native cotton. Not only this, my work also brought to me a rare honour of presenting invited lectures at prestigious International Conferences on 'Cotton Test' held at Faser-Institut in Bremen-Germany, Beltwide Cotton Research Conference in San Diego-USA, World Cotton Research Conference in Athens-Greece, The Second World Textile (AUTEX) Conference in Brugge-Belgium and International Conference on Sustainability of Cotton Production at Dharwad-India.

Epilogue

Endowed with a basic Masters degree in Physics, later a Ph.D. in Fibre Science and Textile Technology and a practical work experience for over 37 years in agricultural research, I personally feel happy, contented, satisfied and amused to have emerged out of an unusual mould called- The Indian Agricultural Research Institute, with a rare combination of qualifications, capability, capacity, experience, knowledge and a broad mental canvas. All that exists within limits from $\mathbf{10^{-14}}$ to $\mathbf{10^{-28}}$ cm, incidentally the universe, interests me with a rare privilege to not only understand but to distinctly see and perceive the undercurrent of universal continuum of creation and connectivity through disciplinary boundaries. Perhaps, it is this realization, visualization, comprehension and knowledge, as I personally see is imaginatively synonymous to what the Gita describes about the 'Grand Vision/Vishwa-roop Darshan' reportedly displayed but nay, factually explained by Shrikrishna to Arjun and nothing more. Shrikrishna was also a human being as others but he was thoughtfully knowledgeable about the fundamental realty of the material continuum explained in the 'Vedas' which precede his time of existence by at least five thousand years. Shrikrishna knew that everything in the material world is created and comes into being from the fundamental units called the 'atoms'. All creations ***(both animate and inanimate)*** arising from the 'atoms' disintegrate into their component atoms over a period of time and are re-cycled by the nature into creating new structures. The meaning of so called 'Vishwaroop Darshan / Grand Vision' is only restricted to explain this fundamental realty in nature.

As a physicist, working in the area of agricultural research, it has been personally, the most fascinating and fulfilling experience of my life. My satisfaction being that my research work was found worthy for nominations to almost all the prestigious national awards for scientific research and excellence besides fellowship of learned academy by the institute authorities on various occasions and they understood and valued it for such merit. My work also earned for me a place of honourable mention and citations in most of the prestigious 'Biographical Compilations' in the world, successively every year for almost a decade. And perhaps the most gratifying being to see my research articles on structure-property relationship in native cotton fibres being classified and mentioned under 'Scholarly Articles' on the Google search engine. The prestigious 'Marathi Vidnyan Parishad' Mumbai, Maharashtra honoured me on 29 th August 2021 with Honourary Life Membership of their organization along with some of the most illustrious scientists of the country. Dr. K. K. Kshirsagar, Honorary Secretary of the nationally known 'Vidnyan Bharati' Pune unit, included me and my research work in the area of 'Agricultural Physics' in his book on 'Praseeddha Bharateeya Krishi-Shastradnya' –Famous Indian Agricultural Scientists', written in Marathi language.

I superannuated from the service in February 2006. The momentum given to my thought process by the institute (IARI) through my active service is still keeping me busy in reading beyond my specialty and writing innovative articles and books ***(see Appendix- List of Publications)*** on topics that broadly fall within the domain of Agricultural Physics and yet take their readers on 'random walks' through apparently unconnected but amazingly inter-connected disciplines. All these articles emphasize the central idea of my life as a 'Physicist in Agricultural Research' that- "All knowledge is a continuum and we must always take a holistic view of any problem for research in hand from a maximum number of inter-connected subject specialties called, disciplines".

डॉ. अनिल विष्णू मोहरीर

यांस,

डॉ. अनिल मोहरीर : जन्म ४ फेब्रुवारी १९४४, नागपूर. आपल्या शालेय शिक्षणाची सुरुवात दिल्ली येथून झाली. भौतिकशास्त्रात १९६५मध्ये बी.एस्सी. आणि १९६७मध्ये एम.एस्सी. पदवी आपण ग्वाल्हेरच्या जिवाजी विद्यापीठामधून प्राप्त केलीत. १९६७मध्ये आपण राष्ट्रीय भौतिक प्रयोगशाळा (एनपीएल)मधून वैज्ञानिक संशोधनाची सुरुवात केली आणि एनपीएलचे तत्कालीन उपसंचालक डॉ. व्ही. जी. भिडे यांच्या मार्गदर्शनाखाली सेलेनिअम फोटोकंडक्टिव्ह सेल्स हा प्रकल्प पूर्ण केलात. आपण इंडियन इन्स्टिट्युट ऑफ टेक्नॉलॉजी, दिल्ली येथून वस्त्रनिर्माणतंत्रातील तंतुमयशास्त्रावर, १९८० यावर्षी पीएच.डी. प्राप्त केलीत.

डिसेंबर १९६८मध्ये भारतीय कृषी संशोधन परिषद (आयसीएआर)मध्ये रुजू झाल्यावर वरिष्ठ संशोधन सहाय्यक, प्राध्यापक आणि विभाग प्रमुख, शास्त्रज्ञ, प्रमुख शास्त्रज्ञ अशा विविध पदांवर कार्यरत होता. कृषी-भौतिकशास्त्र हा वेगळा विषय आपल्या देशात रुजविण्यात आपण बहुमोल कार्य केले आहे. आपण माती, वनस्पती आणि इतर जैविक साहित्याच्या स्पेक्ट्रोस्कोपिक, स्पेक्ट्रो-फोटोमेट्रिक आणि इलेक्ट्रॉन मायक्रोस्कोपिक अभ्यासावर काम करत, त्यातील लोह आणि टायटॅनिअम शोधण्यासाठी अचूक स्पेक्ट्रो-फोटोमेट्रिक पद्धती विकसित केल्या, ज्या आता विश्लेषणात्मक रसायनशास्त्राच्या पाठ्यपुस्तकांमध्ये समाविष्ट आहेत. जैविक साहित्याच्या व्यावहारिक ट्रान्समिशन इलेक्ट्रॉन मायक्रोस्कोपीसाठी अनेक नाविन्यपूर्ण, नमुना प्रक्रिया तंत्रे आपण विकसित केलीत आणि कागद आणि पातळ फिल्म सामग्रीच्या वैशिष्ट्यासाठी 'कॉन्टॅक्ट इलेक्ट्रॉन मायक्रोग्राफी' ही एक नवीन प्रक्रिया पुढे आणली. 'तृणधान्य पिकांच्या बियाण्यांच्या ओलावा हिस्टेरिसिस कर्व्हज'वरील आपल्या अभ्यासाच्या आधारे, कमी पाऊसमान असताना पिकवता येणाऱ्या गहू तसेच तांदळाच्या विविध जाती अधिक पाऊसमान असतानासुद्धा लागवड करण्यासाठी एक सोपी प्रक्रिया आपण विकसित केली आणि 'सामान्यीकृत-ओलावा-हिस्टेरिसिस'ची अभिनव संकल्पना मांडलीत. आपल्या संशोधनाचा प्रत्यक्ष उपयोग बेकरी उत्पादनांचा टिकाऊपणा वाढवण्यासाठी झाला आहे. त्यामध्ये बेल्जिअमच्या डेनॉन बिस्किटांचा प्रामुख्याने उल्लेख करायला हवा.

आपले शंभरहून अधिक शोधनिबंध राष्ट्रीय आणि आंतरराष्ट्रीय नियतकालिकांमध्ये प्रसिद्ध झाले आहेत. जर्मनी, बेल्जिअम आणि अमेरिका या देशांनी आपल्याला भाषणांसाठी निमंत्रित केले होते. अनेक पुस्तकांचे लिखाण, अनुवाद आणि संपादन तसेच सीएसआयआरचे फायबर अँड टेक्सटाइल रिसर्च जर्नल, जर्नल ऑफ एग्रीकल्चर, जर्नल ऑफ एग्रीकल्चरल फिजिक्स या नियतकालिकांकरिता मानद संपादक तसेच मुख्य संपादक म्हणून आपण काम पहिले आहे. निसकॉम-सीएसआयआर यांच्यातर्फे प्रकाशित करण्यात येणाऱ्या ई-पाठ्यपुस्तक प्रकल्पाकरिता नेमलेल्या तज्ज्ञमंडळीमध्ये आपला समावेश होता. आंतरराष्ट्रीय अणुउर्जा संस्था, व्हिएन्ना आणि कमिशन ऑफ युरोपियन कम्युनिटीज, ब्रुसेल्स यांची फेलोशिप आपण मिळवली असून आंतरराष्ट्रीय स्तरावर सहयोगी संशोधन प्रकल्पांमध्ये आपले योगदान आहे. आधुनिक विज्ञान आणि पारंपरिक ज्ञान यांची सांगड घालण्याचे सातत्याने प्रयत्न करणाऱ्या आपल्यासारख्या कृषि-भौतिकशास्त्रज्ञाला मराठी विज्ञान परिषदेचे सन्मान्य सभासदत्व अर्पण करण्यात परिषदेला आनंद तसेच अभिमान वाटत आहे.

प्रा. ज्येष्ठराज भा. जोशी
अध्यक्ष
मराठी विज्ञान परिषद

स्थळ : मुंबई
दिनांक : २९ ऑगस्ट, २०२१

Figure 18: Copy of the Citation-Marathi Vidnyan Parishad

References

1. Ditlevsen, Peter, Henrik Svensmark and Sigfus johnsen, 1996, Contrasting atmospheric and climate dynamics of the last glacial and Holocene periods, Nature, Vol. 379, 810-12.
2. Svensmark, Henrik and Eigil Friis-Christensen, 1997, Variation of cosmic ray flux and global cloud coverage-A missing link in Solar-Climate relationships, Journal of Atmospheric and Solar Terrestrial Physics, Vol. 59, 1225-32.
3. Svensmark, Henrik, 1998, Influence of cosmic rays on Earth's climate, Physical Review Letters, Vol. 81, 5027-30.
4. Marsh, Nigel and Henrik Svensmark, 2000, Low cloud properties influenced by cosmic rays, Physical Review Letters, Vol. 85, 5004-07.
5. Marsh, Nigel and Henrik Svensmark, 2000, Cosmic rays, clouds and climate, Space Science Review, Vol. 94, 215-30.
6. Svensmark, Henrik, 2003, Cosmic rays and the evolution of Earth's climate during the last 4.6 billion years, e-print http://arxiv.org/abs/physics/0311087.
7. Svensmark, Henrik, Jens Olaf Pepke Pedersen, Nigel Marsh, Martin Enghoff and Ulrik Uggerhoj, 2007, Experimental evidence for the role of ions in particle nucleation under atmospheric conditions, Proceedings of the Royal Society A, Vol. 463, 385-96.
8. Svensmark, Henrik and Nigel Calder, 2007, The Chilling Stars-A New Theory of Climate Change, ICON Books.
9. Vartak P. V. The Scientific Dating of Ramayana and the Vedas, 1999, Ved Vidnyana Mandal, 497, Shaniwar Peth, Pune-30, India
10. Vartak, P. V. The Scientific Dating of the Mahabharata War, Ved Vidnyana Mandal, 497, Pune-30, India
11. Moharir, A.V., Issues about atmospheric and fertilizer nitrogen, global warming and urgent priorities, University News, a Weekly Journal of Higher Education, Published by the association of Indian Universities, New Delhi, Vol. 49 No. 27, July 04-10, 2011, 09-18.Also abstracted for Poster Presentation at the International Nitrogen Conference N2010, New Delhi 2010.

12. Waradpande, N.R., 'The Nemesis of Nehru-Worship' Sahitya Sindhu Prakashan, Bangalore, India, 2001.
13. Vartak, P. V. Upanishadanchey Vaidnyana-Nishtha Nirupan (In Marathi) Vol. I & II, 521 Shaniwar Peth, Pune-411030, India.
14. Guney, M. R. Dnyaneshwareechey Bhava-Vishwa (In Marathi), Snehal Prakashan, Pune-411030, India.
15. Chandrashekhar, S., 'Newton's Principia for the Common Reader', Oxford University Press, USA, 2003.
16. Moharir, A.V. et.al Editor, 'Four Decades of Research in Agricultural Physics'(1962-2002), Division of Agricultural Physics, Indian Agricultural Research Institute, New Delhi 2003.
17. Moharir, A.V. Editor, 'PROFILE IN SOLITUDE-Professor A.B. Joshi *(B.17 November 1916, Jabalpur, India)* Felicitation on his Ninety First Birthday.
18. Moharir, A. V., B. C. Panda and V. B. Gupta, Polarizing Microscopic Study of the Origin and Growth of Extinction Bands in Native Cotton Fibres, Indian J. Text. Res. 1986, Vol. 11, 1-6.
19. Moharir, A.V., Lieva Van Langenhove and Paul Kiekens, Convolutions in the same diploid and tetraploid cotton varieties grown at different agroclimatic locations, Paper Orally Presented at the Beltwide Cotton Production Research Conference, January 5-9, 1998, San Diego, California, U.S.A. Proc. Beltwide Cotton Prod. Res. Conf. Vol 2, pp 1587-1592.
20. Moharir, A. V. An investigation of the structure and mechanical properties of cotton fibres of *Gossypium hirsutum* species with Emphasis on evolving a suitable parameter for varietal screening, Ph. D. Thesis, Indian Institute of Technology, New Delhi, 1980.
21. Gupta, V. B., A. V. Moharir and B. C. Panda, Characterization of some Indian cotton varieties by X-Ray diffraction and electron microscopic techniques and correlation of their structure and mechanical properties, 'Cotton In a Competitive World', Monograph, Ed. P. W. Harrison, The Textile Institute, Manchester, England, 1979, pp 83-106.
22. Moharir, A. V., Manish Bodas and Ananta Vashisth, Rate and amount of cellulose synthesis in developing fibres of *Gossypium arboretum and Gossypium hirsutum* cotton. Journal of Applied Polymer Science, Vol. 90 No. 6, 2003, 1453-1462.
23. Moharir, A.V., Structure and Strength-Crystallite Orientation Relationship in Native Cotton Fibres (Research cum Review Article), Indian Journal of Fibre and Textile Research, Vol. 12, June 1987, pp 106-119.
24. Moharir, A.V. and Paul Kiekens, Cellulose crystallite sizes in diploid and tetraploid native cotton, Journal of Applied Polymer Science, 1998, Vol. 68, pp 2107-2112.
25. Moharir, A. V., Lieva Van Langenhove, Els Van Nimmen, Johanna Louwagie and Paul Kiekens, True spiral angles in diploid and tetraploid native cotton fibres grown

at different locations, Journal of Applied Polymer Science, Vol. 70, No. 10, 1998, 303-310.

26. Moharir, A. V., Lieva Van Langenhove, Els Van Nimmen, Johanna Louwagie and Paul Kiekens, Stability of X-Ray cellulose crystallite orientation parameters in native cotton with change of location and year of growth, Journal of Applied Polymer Science, Vol. 72, No. 2, 1999, 269-276.

Photographs of Some Selected Memorable Events

Padmashri Dr. A. B. Joshi, Director-IARI with Dr. A. V. Moharir

"Always try to go higher and higher;
There is always room at the top".
Writes Dr. A. B. Joshi, Director-IARI in my autograph book

Chief Election Commissioner Mr. T. N. Seshan, Prof. Dr. Ram Badan Singh, Director-IARI and Dr. A. V. Moharir, Secretary Pusa Agril Res. Sci. Soc.

L to R: Professor Dr. Ashok K, Sarbhoy, President, Pusa Agril. Res. Sci. Soc., Professor Dr. Ram Badan Singh, Director-IARI, Dr. Raghunath A. Mashelkar, Director General, C.S.I.R. and Dr. A. V. Moharir, Secretary, Pusa Agril. Res. Sci. Soc.

Dr. Charudatta D. Mayee, Chairman, Agricultural Scientists Recruitment Board (ASRB) in center, releasing the book-'Profile in Solitude' on 17-11-2007 with Dr. V. S. P. Rao, Director, Agharkar Research Institute, in the auditorium of the Agharkar Institute, Pune

L to R: Dr. Arvind S. Summanwar, Dr. V. S. P. Rao, Dr. C. D. Mayee, Dr. A. V. Moharir, Mr. Jayant Atmaram Joshi (S/O Dr. A. B. Joshi) and Dr. Y. S. Nerkar, Vice Chancellor, MPKV, Rahuri, Maharashtra, present on the occasion.

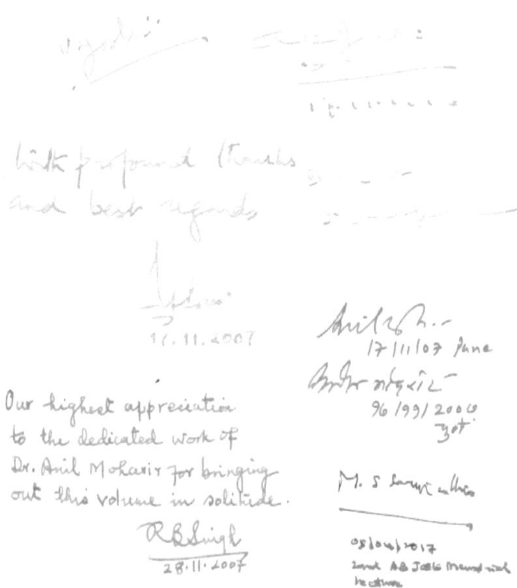

First Copy of the book- 'Profile In Solitude, Professor A. B. Joshi: Felicitation on his Ninety First Birthday, Dated 17-11-2007, Edited by A. V. Moharir, autographed after its release in Pune by Mrs. Vimal Atmaram Joshi (W/O Dr. A. B. Joshi), Dr. Atmaram Bhairav (A. B.) Joshi, Mr. Jayant Atmaram Joshi, Prof. Dr. M. S. Swaminathan, Professor Dr. R. B. Singh and Dr. A. V. Moharir.

Shri Rajiv Gandhi, then General Secretary of the Congress party with Dr. A. V. Moharir

Dr. A P J Abdul Kalam, then Principal Scientific Advisor to the Defence Minister, Government of India with Dr. Anil V. Moharir and Mr Krishna Chandra Aeron, Editor-Business Inn Journal presenting a copy of the Issue of the Journal that Printed the first ever Review on Dr. Kalam's autobiographical book- "WINGS OF FIRE" written by Dr. A. V. Moharir. *(Business Inn Journal, Vol. 20, No. 1, pp 28-30, 1999).*

Mr Mukund Shankar (M.S.) Kirloskar, India's prominent industrialist with Dr. A. V. Moharir

Professor Dr. Pramod Kumar Chhonkar, FNAAS, President, Indian Society of Soil Science with Dr. A. V. Moharir

Professor Dr. Ravin Lakshman Thatte, FRCS (Edin) India's most pioneering and renowned plastic and reconstructive surgeon and an authoritative writer on 'Dnyaneshwari' the immortal commentary on 'Gita' written by Sant Dnyaneshwar, with Dr. A. V. Moharir

Professor Dr. Padmanabhan Balaram, former Director, Indian Institute of Science, Bengaluru, Dr. A. V. Moharir and Professor Dr. Prameela Krishnan, Head-Division of Agricultural Physics-IARI

Appendix

- **List of Publications of Professor Anil Vishnu Moharir**

1. Spectrophotometric determination of iron with Orthophenanthroline.
   G. S. R. Krishnamurti, A. V. Moharir and V. A. K. Sarma,
   Microchemical J., 1970, Vol.15, 585-589.
2. Analytical emission spectroscopy.
   A. V. Moharir,
   Science Reporter, 1971, Vol. 8, 528-530.
3. Spectrophotometric determination of Titanium with 'Trion'.
   A. V. Moharir, V. A. K. Sarma and G. S. R. Krishnamurti,
   Microchemical J., 1972, Vol. 17, 167-172.
4. Spectrophotometric determination of phosphorus with ascorbic acid as a reductant,
   A. V. Moharir, G. S. R. Krishnamurti and V. A. K. Sarma. (Unpublished method).
5. Replication of surface features of sand grains of sizes 0.5 to 4 mm for electron microscopy,
   A. V. Moharir and Nam Prakash,
   Current Science,1974, Vol. 43, 323-324.
6. Formvar films and nets for electron microscopy,
   A. V. Moharir and Nam Prakash
   J. Physics (E) Sci. Instruments. 1975, Vol. 8, 288-290.
7. Cotton fibre surface replicas for electron microscopy,
   A. V. Moharir, B. C. Panda
   Indian J. Textile Res., 1976, Vol. 1, 64-66.
8. Potentialities of carbon surface replicas for varietal characterization of cotton fibres: An electron microscope study,
   A. V. Moharir, B. C. Panda, and V. B. Gupta
   J. Nuclear Agril. & Biol, 1978, Vol. 7, 72-74.

9. Studies on the mossaic disease of musk melon (cucumis melo-L),
T. K. Nariani, S. M. Viswanath, S. P. Raychoudhuri and A. V. Moharir,
Current Science,1977, Vol. 46, 47-48.
10. Witch's broom of cowpea-A mycoplasmal disease,
Varma, S. R. Sharma and A. V. Moharir,
Current Science,1978, Vol. 47, 56-57.
11. Isolation of spirilum Lipoferum from stems of wheat and Nitrogen fixation in enrichment cultures,
S. K. Kavimandan, N. S. Subbarao and A. V. Moharir,
Current Science, 1978, Vol. 47, 96-98.
12. Electron Microscope: How did it evolve? ,
A. V. Moharir,
Science Reporter, 1977, Vol. 14, 280-294.
13. Characterization of some Indian cotton varieties by X-ray diffraction and electron microscopic techniques and correlation of their structure and mechanical properties.
V. B. Gupta, A. V. Moharir and B. C. Panda,
"Cotton in a Competitive World" Monograph, Ed. P.W. Harrison, The Textile Institute, Manchester, England, (1979) pp 83-106.
14. Convolutions and reversals in cotton fibre,
A. V. Moharir, B. C. Panda and V. B. Gupta,
J. Textile Inst., 1979, Vol. 70, 457-459.
15. Dependence of stiffness and strength of *Gossypium hirsutum* cotton on crystallite Orientation,
A. V. Moharir, B. C. Panda, V. B. Gupta, K. C. Nagpal and D. K. Suri,
Textile Res. J., 1980, Vol. 50, 596-600.
16. An Investigation of the structure and mechanical properties of cotton fibres of *Gossypium hirsutum* species with emphasis on evolving a suitable parameter for varietal screening,
A. V. Moharir,
Ph.D. Thesis, Indian Institute of Technology, New Delhi (1980).
17. Purification and serology of cowpea (Vigna Sinensis Savi) mossaic Virus,
T. K. Nariani, S. M. Viswanath, V. V. Chenulu and A. V. Moharir,
Current Science, 1980, Vol. 49, 680-681.
18. Regulation of starch synthesis and starch ultra structure in high lysine mutant of Barley,
S. L. Mehta, Kavita Sood , Nam Prakash and A. V. Moharir,
Paper presented at the 57th annual meeting of society of Biological chemists, November 18-20, 1982, Chandigarh, India.

19. Starch ultra structure in developing grains of high lysine barley mutants,
Kavita Sood, A. V. Moharir, Nam Prakash, and S. L. Mehta,
Paper presented at 57th annual meeting of society of Biological chemists, November 18-20, 1982, Chandigarh, India.
20. X-ray characterization of cotton for strength,
K. C. Nagpal, D. K. Suri, B. C. Panda, K. M. Vijayraghvan, and A. V. Moharir,
Paper presented at the 13th National seminar on crystallography, Nagpur University, Nagpur, March 15-18, 1982.
21. Dependence of stiffness and strength of cotton fibres on crystallite Orientation
A. V. Moharir, K. M. Vijayraghvan, B. C. Panda and V. B. Gupta,
Proceedings International Conference on "Cotton Test" Faserinstitute, Bremen, West Germany, January 21-23, 1982. Also Textile Res.J. 1982, Vol. 52, 756-760.
22. X-ray varietal characterization of cotton of the *Gossypium arboreum* species for strength,
K. M. Vijayraghvan, A. V. Moharir, B. C. Panda, K. C. Nagpal, D. K. Suri and V. B. Gupta,
J., Textile Inst., 1983, Vol. 74, 38-43.
23. Structural dependence of some mechanical properties of cotton of the *Gossypium hirsutum* species,
V. B. Gupta, A. V. Moharir and B. C. Panda,
J. Textile Inst.,1984, Vol. 75, 243-251.
24. Characterization of cotton during dehydration phase,
B. C. Panda, K. M. Vijayraghvan, A. V. Moharir, V. K. Gupta and Munshi Singh,
Annales of Agril. Res., 1984, 543-51.
25. Establishment of single phase structural model for cotton cellulose from X-ray diffraction studies,
A. V. Moharir, B. C. Panda and V. B. Gupta,
Paper presented at the 16th National Seminar on Crystallography, January 2-4 (1985) Department of Physics, University of Delhi.
26. Some observations on the origin and growth of extinction bands in native cotton fibres through polarized microscope,
A. V. Moharir, B. C. Panda, and V. B. Gupta
Paper presented at the 13th National Symposium on optics and Opto-Electronics, February 5-8, (1986), National Physical Laboratory, New Delhi, India.
27. Polarizing microscopic study of the origin and growth of extinction bands in native cotton fibres,
A. V. Moharir, B. C. Panda and V. B. Gupta,
Indian J. Text. Res. 1986, Vol. 11, 1-6.

28. Crystallite orientation in some cotton varieties of *Gossypium* barbadense,
A. V. Moharir, K. M. Vijayraghvan, B. C. Panda, D. K. Suri and K. C. Nagpal,
Indian J. Textile Res.,1986, Vol. 11, 82-85.
29. Crystallite orientation in some cotton varieties of *Gossypium herbaceum* ,
A. V. Moharir, K. M. Vijayraghvan, B. C. Panda, D. K. Suri, and K. C. Nagpal
Indian J, Textile Res., 1986, Vol. 11, 117-120.
30. Structure and strength crystallite orientation relationship in native cotton fibres
: A Review Article,
A. V. Moharir,
Indian J. Textile Res., 1987, Vol. 12, 106-119.
31. Low cost solar dehydration chamber for drying cotton fibers,
B. C. Panda and A. V. Moharir,
Paper presented at the National Symposium on use of radiations and radioisotopes in agriculture, biology and animal science with special emphasis on post harvest technology and animal vaccine production, Indian society for Nuclear Tech. in Agril. And Biol., Srinagar, J, & K. May 22- 25, 1985.
32. Modification of surface properties of formvar substrates for electron microscopy
A. V. Moharir and Nam Prakash,
Proceedings 2nd international symposium on Biophysics and Electron microscopy 'Biophysics and electron microscopy' Ed, S. R. Bawa, Department of Biophysics, Punjab University, Chandigarh, India pp. 299-304, 1986. Also in Indian J., Biochem and Biophysics. 1986, Vol. 23, 283- 285.
33. Contact electron micrography for characterization of paper : A New Technique
A. V. Moharir and Nam Prakash,
Current Science, 1988, Vol. 57, 391-393.
34. Contact electron micrography for characterization of paper in a transmission electron microscope: A New technique,
A. V. Moharir and Nam Prakash
J. Materials Science, 1988, Vol. 23, 3843-3846.
35. Cotton : The wonderful natural fibre,
A. V. Moharir,
Science Reporter (C.S.I.R) 1989, Vol. 26 (2) , 87-90.
36. Electron microscope turns 50 (An Invited Article),
A. V. Moharir,
Science Reporter (C.S.I.R) 26 (10) (1989) 552-558.
37. Domestic laundering of clothes and washing machines,
A. V. Moharir,
Science Reporter (C.S.I.R) 1991 (Submitted and could not be published)

38. Possibility of inducing beneficial effects to wheat plants through subjecting its seeds to extreme vacuum desiccation,
    K. Roy, A. V. Moharir and B. C. Panda,
    Paper presented at the National Symposium on Vacuum Science and technology, Indian Vacuum Society and Center for Advanced Technology, Indore, Madhya Pradesh, November 13-15, 1991.
39. NMR analysis of seed oil content in ginned and acid-delinted samples of certain diploid and tetraploid cotton cultivars,
    P. N. Gambhir and A. V. Moharir,
    J. Indian Soc. Cotton Improv.,1997 : 38-40.
40. Origin and growth of extinction bands in native cotton fibres,
    A. V. Moharir and Paul Kiekens,
    Indian Textile J., 1992, Vol. 102, 110-115.
41. Questions about constancy of True-spiral angle in cotton?
    A. V. Moharir,
    J. Appl. Polymer Sci., 1992, Vol. 44, 1121-1124.
42. The correlation between X-ray orientation parameters and strength of fibres in native cotton,
    A. V. Moharir, Johanna Louwagie, Lieva van Langenhove and Paul Kiekens,
    J. Appl. Polymer Sci., 1992 , Vol. 44, 1913- 1919.
43. The correlation of X-ray orientation parameters with strength of cotton fibres and the genetic inheritance of orientation parameters in inter-specific F1 hybrids,
    A. V. Moharir, K. M. Vijayraghvan, B. C. Panda, and Munshi Singh, Paper presented at the Silver Jubilee Symposium of the All India Coordinated Cotton Improvement Project, Coimbatore, September 17-19,1992.
44. True spiral angle in cotton of *Gossypium arboreum,*
    A. V. Moharir and K. M. Vijayraghvan,
    J. Appl. Polymer Sci. 1993, Vol. 48,1869-1872.
45. Nature of resistance to cucumber green motile mossaic virus (CGMMV) in melons (cucumis spp),
    L. Rajamony, T. A. More, V. S. Sheshadri and A. V. Moharir
    Proceedings 6th Kerala Science Congress, January 1994, Thiruanantapuram, pp 364-366, sponsored by Department of Science and Technology, Govt. of India
46. Moisture desorption and absorption isotherms for seeds of some cultivars of *Triticum aestivum* and *Triticum durum* wheats,
    A. V. Moharir
    Paper presented at the DAE-BRNS Symposium on nuclear Applications in agriculture, animal husbandry and food-preservation, March 16-18, 1994, N.R.L., I.A.R.I., New Delhi, Proc. pp. 181-185.

47. Moisture desorption and absorption isotherms for seeds of some cultivars of *Triticum durum* and *Triticum aestivum* wheats,
A. V. Moharir and Nam Prakash
Current Science, 1995, Vol. 68, 316-326.
48. Moisture desorption and absorption isotherms for seeds of some cultivars of *Triticum dicoccum* wheat,
A. V. Moharir
Current Science 1996, Vol.70 No. 11, 1012-1017
49. Moisture hysteresis curves for seeds of *Triticum aestivum, durum* and *dicoccum* wheats, their variations and probable laboratory procedure for screening genotypes for rainfed cultivation,
A. V. Moharir,
2nd International Crop Science Congress, New Delhi, India Nov. 17-24, 1996 , poster presentation Abstract no.P-3-053.
50. The interfibrillar phase in poly (ethylene terapathalate) fibre,
V. B. Gupta, A. K. Jain, A. V. Moharir and Nam Prakash,
Polymer (1997) Vol. 38 , 3713-3715.
51. X-ray crystallite orientation in native cotton fibres,
A. V. Moharir, K. M. Vijayraghavan and Paul Kiekens ,
Paper presented at the DAE-BRNS National Symposium on Nuclear Techniques in increasing crop and animal productivity.
Indian society for Nuclear Techniques In Agriculture and Biology, October 7-9 1996, Mumbai-India. Also in Indian J. Fibre and Text Res. (1997) Vol. 22, 141-145.
52. NMR seed-oil content in certain diploid and tetraploid cotton cultivars in ginned and acid delinted samples,
P. N. Gambhir and A. V. Moharir,
J. Indian Soc. For Cotton Improv. (1997) Vol. 22, 38-40.
53. The Development and Structure of Cotton Fibre : The Wonderful Gift of nature.
A. V. Moharir,
Business Inn Journal, 1998, 21, 5-8.
54. Structure and determinants of fibre strength in native cotton,
A. V. Moharir, A. B. Dongre and Lieva Van Langenhove,
Second World Cotton Research Conference, September 5-12,1998, Athens, Greece (ABSTRACT BOOK, Abstract No. 328, page No. 335).
55. Cellulose crystallite sizes in diploid and tetraploid native cotton,
A. V. Moharir and Paul Kiekens,
J. Appl. Polymer Sci. (1998) Vol. 68, 2107-2112.

56. Convolutions in the same diploid and tetraploid cotton varieties grown at different agroclimatic locations,
Anil V. Moharir, Lieva Van Langenhove and Paul Kiekens
Paper Orally Presented at the Beltwide Cotton Production Research Conference, January 5-9, 1998, San Diego, California, U.S.A.
Proc. Beltwide Cotton Prod. Res. Conf. Vol 2, pp 1587-1592.
57. The Origin and growth of extinction bands in cotton,
Anil V. Moharir , Lieva Van Langenhove and Paul Kiekens,
Paper Orally Presented at the Beltwide Cotton Production Research Conference, January 5-9, 1998 , San Diego, California, U.S.A.
Proc. Beltwide Cotton Prod. Res. Conf. Vol.2, pp 1583-1587.
58. True spiral angles in diploid and tetraploid native cotton fibres grown at different Locations,
A. V. Moharir, Lieva Van Langenhove, Johanna Louwagie, Els Van Nimmen, and Paul Kiekens,
J. Applied Polym. Sci., 1998, Vol.70, 303-310.
59. Stability of X-ray cellulose crystallite orientation parameters in native cotton With change of location and year of growth,
A. V. Moharir, Lieva Van Langenhove, Els Van Nimmen, Johanna Louwagie, and Paul Kiekens
J. Applied Polym. Sci., 1999, Vol.72, 269-276.
60. Paper in preparation : Moisture desorption and absorption isotherms and normalized hysteresis curves for seeds as parameter for screening wheat cultivars for rainfed agriculture.
A. V. Moharir,
Business Inn Journal (1999)
61. Dr. Bhikari Charan Panda: An Individual and a Teacher par excellence
A. V. Moharir,
Felicitation Write up on the eve of his retirement from service. April 30, 1999.
62. Structure and determinants of fibre strength in native cotton fibre,
A. V. Moharir,
Indian J. Fibre & Text. Res. 2000 25, 1-7.
63. My First Interaction with a Bharat Ratna,
A. V. Moharir,
Business Inn Journal 1999.
64. An Approach paper for promoting communal harmony,
A. V. Moharir and P. K. Singh,
National Foundation for Communal Harmony, Government of India.

65. Note on the Internationalization of Higher Education, Note prepared for use of the Dean-Indian Agricultural Research Institute.
66. Emotional World of Bharat Ratna A. P. J. Abdul Kalam,
A. V. Moharir
Vistas of India : Oracles in Tourism, Business Inn Journal Vol 2, 2001, pp 327-328.
67. Multidisciplinary Approach in Agricultural Research and Education : Need of the Time.
Akshayber Singh and A. V. Moharir,
University News (2001) 39 (49) 10-15.
68. Rate and Amount of Cellulose Synthesis in developing fibres of *Gossypium arboreum* and *Gossypium hirsutum* cotton,
A. V. Moharir, Manish Bodas and Ananta Vashisth,
Journal of Applied Polymer Science (2003) 90(6) 1453-1462.
69. Structure and Structure-Property Relationship in Native Cotton : Some Challenges to Breeders : Key Note Address
A. V. Moharir
The Second World Textile (AUTEX) Conference, Bruges-Belgium, 1-3 rd July 2002, Proceedings of the Conference, pp 493-516.
70. Emotional World of Bharat Ratna APJ Abdul Kalam
A. V. Moharir
Vistas of India, Oracles in Tourism, Ed. Kamalesh Deka, Business Inn Publication (2002), Special Issue on North East India).Vol. 2, pp 237-238
71. Strengthening Multidisciplinary Approach in Agricultural Education : Need For Change.
A. Singh and A. V. Moharir,
University News (2001) 39 (49) 10- 15.
72. Structure and Structure-Property Relationship in Native Cotton: Some Challenges to Breeders , A Review Article,
A. V. Moharir
Indian J. Fibre & Text. Res. (2003) 28, 348-362.
73. Characterization of wheat (*Triticum aestivum*) and soybean (*Glycine max*) seeds under accelerated ageing conditions by proton nuclear magnetic resonance (NMR) spectroscopy.
P. Krishnan, S. Nagarajan, M. Dadlani and A. V. Moharir.
Seed Sci. & Technology, (2003) 31, 541-550.
74. Characterization of germination and non-viable wheat seeds by nuclear magnetic resonance (NMR) spectroscopy.
P. Krishnan, D. K. Joshi, Shantha Nagarajan and A. V. Moharir,
European Biophysics Journal (2004) 33, 76-82.

75. Characterization of soybean and wheat seeds by Nuclear Magnetic Resonance Spectroscopy.
    P. Krishnan, D. K. Joshi, M. Maheshwari, S. Nagarajan, and A. V. Moharir,
    Biologia Plantarum (2004) 48, 117-120.
76. Changes in NMR relaxation times in soybean and wheat seeds equilibrated at different temperatures and relative humidity.
    P. Krishnan, S. Nagarajan and A.V. Moharir
    Indian J. Biochem. & Biophys. (2003) 40, 46-50.
77. Cellulose synthesis and physical properties of fibres of *Gossypium hirsutum* and *Gossypium arboreum* varieties.
    Ananta Vashisth, A. V. Moharir and Shilpi Kulshrestha
    Proc. Symp.on Geoinformatics Applications for Sustainable Development, New Delhi, February 17-19, 2004, pp 363-369.
78. Characterization of germinating and non-viable soybean seeds by nuclear magnetic resonance (NMR) spectroscopy
    P. Krishnan, D. K. Joshi, Shantha Nagarajan and A. V. Moharir
    Seed Science Research (2004) 14, 355-362.
79. Thermodynamic characterization of seed deterioration during storage under accelerated ageing conditions
    P. Krishnan, Shantha Nagarajan and A. V. Moharir
    Biosystems Engineering (2004) 89(4), 425-433.
80. Cellulose synthesis and physical properties of fibres of Gossypium hirsutum and Gossypium arboretum varieties.
    Ananta Vashisth, A. V. Moharir and Shilpi Kulshrestha
    Proceedings of the Symposium on Geoinformatics Applications for Sustainable Development, I.A.R.I., New Delhi, February 17-19, 2004, pp 363-369.
81. Physics in agriculture and Agricultural physics as a profession.
    A. V. Moharir
    'University News', A Weekly Journal of Higher Education, Association of Indian Universities, New Delhi, Vol 43 (06), 2005, 7-12 & 18.
82. A discussion on the requisites on raw cotton fibre properties for high-speed spinning and practical approach for breeding new varieties with inherent high fibre tenacity.
    A. V. Moharir (Invited Speaker)
    Paper Presented at the International Symposium on Strategies for Sustainable Cotton Production: A Global Vision, University of Agricultural Sciences, Dharwad, Karnataka, November 23-25, 2004, Proceedings of the Symposium Vol. 1, Crop Improvement, pp 61-67.
83. Light Optical and Electron Microscopic Studies on Cotton Fibre Development and Structure.
    A. V. Moharir

Lead Paper Presented at the National Seminar on Improvement of Fibre Quality Traits in Cotton, Proceedings, February 15, 2005, Central Institute of Cotton Research, Nagpur, pp 118-126.

84. Issues about Atmospheric and Fertilizer Nitrogen, Global Warming and Urgent Priorities 'Opinion Article'
A. V. Moharir
'University News', A Weekly Journal of Higher Education, Association of Indian Universities, New Delhi, 'Special Issue on Environmental Issues and Global Warming', 2007, October 29-Nov. 04, Vol. 45, No. 44, pp 131-137.
85. Our Cosmic Relationships, Food Nutrients and Good Health: An Attempted Syntheses
A. V. Moharir
'University News', A Weekly Journal of Higher Education, Association of Indian Universities, New Delhi, Vol. 45, No. 28, July 9-15, 2007.
86. Research paper writing skill in effective writing and communication
A. V. Moharir
Current Science, Vol. 93, No. 1, July 10, 2007, p 6-7.
87. Post Graduate School System of the Indian Agricultural Research Institute, New Delhi: A note on appraisal and suggestive agenda for future progress.
A. V. Moharir
University News, A Weekly Journal of Higher Education, Association of Indian Universities, Vol. 46, No.46, 2008, pp 79-85. Special Issue on Higher Education (Agriculture)
88. Science and Spirituality
A.V. Moharir
University News, a Weekly Journal of Higher Education of the Association of Indian Universities, Vol. 46 No. 52, December 29, 2008 -January 04, 2009, pp 13-15. Also Moderately Edited version of the article Reproduced in part in 'Akhand Gyan', A publication of the Divya Jagrati Sansthan, New Delhi, February 2009, Vol. 2, No. 2, pp 13-15.
89. The Twentieth Century Generation Members of the Thakar Family from Pune : Personalities I met and admired *(A Commemorative Booklet on Six Thakar Brothers and their Sister)*
A. V. Moharir
Published by the author, January 1, 2009, pp 20. (For Private Circulation only)
90. Agricultural Physics and Integrative Biology
A. V. Moharir
University News, A Weekly Journal of Higher Education of the Association of Indian Universities, Vol. 47, No. 43, (Oct 26-Nov 01), pp 10-13, 2009.

91. Scientific interpretation of the concept of 'Sapta Lok' seven heavens and 'Sapta Paatal' seven hells from ancient Indian philosophy.
P. V. Gokhale
Translated in English from original in Marathi and re-presented with minor editing and annotations for wider discussion amongst scientific community By
A. V. Moharir
Abridged version of the article published in 'Akhand Gyan' A monthly international publication of the Divya Jagrity Sansthan, Pitampura, New Delhi, February, pp 13-15 & 26, 2010.
Also Published in Journal of Literature, Culture and Media Studies, Vol. II. 3 Jan-Jun, 2010, pp 208-219. Also to be published in the Journal of Asian Agri-History Foundation 2013.
92. Through the apparent nature: A random walk in solitude,
A. V. Moharir
University News, A Weekly Journal of Higher Education Published by the Association of Indian Universities, Vol 48 No. 16, April 19-25, 2010, pp 19-25.
93. Science, spirituality and God : An attempted Syntheses
A. V. Moharir
University News, A Weekly Journal of Higher Education, Association of Indian Universities, Vol. 48 No. 39, September 27-October 03, 2010, pp 37-43.
94. Professor Anupam Varma as I know him
A. V. Moharir
Souvenir published on the occasion of one day Seminar on 'Role of Transgenics in Shaping Indian Agriculture' to commemorate 70 th Birthday of Professor Anupam Varma, organized by the Indian Virological Society, Indian Agricultural Research Institute, New Delhi, July 23 rd, 2010, pp 35-36.
95. Form of Motion of Matter : A Kaleiodoscope of Physics in Life
A. V. Moharir
Journal of Agricultural Physics, Vol. 7, No. 1-2, 2007, pp 1-7.
96. Form of Motion of Matter : The Foundation of Quality Higher Education
A. V. Moharir
An Invited article for the Souvenir released on the eve of UGC-AIU All India Vice Chancellors' Conference and 85 th Annual Meeting of the Association of Indian Universities, Bharati Vidyapeeth, Deemed University, Pune, November 12-14, 2010, pp 67-73. Also published in University News, A weekly journal of higher education, published by the Association of Indian Universities, Vol. 49, No. 02, January 10-16, 2011, pp 1-6.
97. Work: Its Origin, Law and Human Obligations
A. V. Moharir

University News, A weekly journal of higher education, published by the Association of Indian Universities, Vol. 49, No. 03, January 17- 24, 2011, pp 13-17.

98. Issues about Atmospheric and Fertilizer Nitrogen, Global Warming and Urgent Priorities-II
A. V. Moharir
University News, A Weekly journal of higher education, published by the Association of Indian Universities, Vol. 49 No. 27, July 04-10, 2011, pp 9-18.
Also as Poster Abstract presented at the N2010, 5 th International Nitrogen Conference, December 3-7, New Delhi, India vide Poster Abstracts- Climate Change N2010/Part/cc/P515, Book of Abstracts Page No. 367. Organized by the Indian Nitrogen Group and the Society for Conservation of Nature in association with the International Nitrogen Initiative.

99. Quantum Physics and New Biology: The Emerging Paradigm Change
A. V. Moharir
Journal of Agricultural Physics, 2011, Vol. 11, 1-12.
Also Reproduced in 'University News' Weekly Journal of Higher Education, Association of Indian Universities, Vol 50 No. 13 March 26-April 01, 2012, pp 6-15.

100. Dr. RAMCHANDRA JAIKRISHNA (R. J.) KALAMKAR - A Leader of Indian Agriculture (BIOGRAPHY)
A. V. Moharir
Asian Agri-History Foundation , Vol. 17, July-Sept. 2013, pp 287-293.

101. MADHUKAR NARAYAN PAITHANKAR (BIOGRAPHY)
A Trainers Trainer in Agricultural and Rural Extension Services)
A. V. Moharir
Asian Agri-History Foundation, Vol. 18, No. 1, 2014, pp 69-74..

102. ATMARAM BHAIRAV JOSHI (BIOGRAPHY)
A. V. Moharir
MEMOIRES OF FELLOWS- Indian National Scientific Academy, Bahadur Shah Zaffar Marg, New Delhi- 110 002, Vol. 39, 2011 pp 154-169.
Also for the Memoirs of Fellows of the National Academy of Agricultural Sciences, DP Shastri Marg, New Delhi-110012, 2011.

103. A New Theory of Cloud Formation and Climate Change on the Earth
A. V. Moharir
As Editorial Commentry, Journal of Agricultural Physics, Vol. 12, No. 2, 1-12, 2012. Also reproduced in University News. A Weekly Journal of Higher Education published by the Association of Indian Universities, Vol. 50, No. 28, July 09-15, 2012, pp 18-24.
Journal of Agricultural Physics, Vol. 12, No. 2, 2012, pp 91-99.

104. Biocentrism : Scientific Evidence of Life-After Death
A. V. Moharir
NAAS NEWS, Vol 13, No 4, October-December 2014, pp 16-17, National Academy of Agricultural Sciences, New Delhi. Also published under modified and enlarged article title *'Biocentrism: A Future Area of Research' in the University News, A Weekly Journal of Higher Education, published by the Association of Indian Universities, New Delhi, Vol. 51, No. 49, December 09-15, 2013).*

105. A Scientific Look at the Soul: An Attempted Synthesis
A. V. Moharir
University News, A Weekly Journal of Higher Education, Published by the Association of Indian Universities, New Delhi. Vol. 52 No. 29, July 21-27, 2014, pp 19-30.

106. A Scientific Look at the Concept of Soul : Attempted Synthesis
A. V. Moharir
Paper Presented at the 88 th Session of the Indian Philosophical Congress, S V University, Tirupati, Andhra Pradesh, India, October 17-19, 2014.

107. Questions about Soul and Re-birth: Need for Fresh Look and Re-definition
A. V. Moharir
Paper Presented at the National Conference on Ancient Science and Technology:Retrospection and Aspirations (ASTRA-2015), Fergusson College, University of Pune, January 10-11, 2015. And Published in the Special Issue of 'TATWADEEP' brought out on the eve of the conference. Also submitted for publication in the University News, Weekly Journal of Higher Education, published by the Association of Indian Universities, New Delhi (January 2015).

108. Science Spirituality and God : An Attempted Syntheses
Anil Vishnu Moharir
Reprinted from the 'University News', A Weekly Journal of Higher Education, Published by the Association of Indian Universities, Vol. 56 No. 40, October 01-07, 2018, pp 18-24.

109. Expectations and the Delusion on the Behaviour of Teachers: Some Random Thoughts.
Anil Vishnu Moharir
Reprinted from the University News, A Weekly Journal of Higher Education, Published by the Association of Indian Universities, Vol. 56 No. 43, October 22-28, 2018 pp 7-12.

110. Random Thoughts on the Eve of 69 th Republic Day of India on January 26, 2019: Delusions and Expectations. (Communicated to the University News, March 06, 2019, for possible publication)..
A. V. Moharir

111. Professor Dr. Bhikari Charan Panda,
A Scientist, Philosopher, Scholar and Teacher Par Excellence (Unpublished)
112. The Most Scientific 'Sanatan Vedic Philosophy' is the only Option before Humanity for Peace, Progress, Salvation and Continued Existence on the Earth.
A. V. Moharir
(Random Thoughts. Widely circulated through e-Mail and Whats App. Circulated Document. December 2020.
Also published in 'In Quest of Bharateeya Shikshan' A Bi-monthly magazine of the Maharashtra Bharateeya Shikshan Mandal, Mumbai, Vol 30, Issue No. 04, July-August 2021, pp 25-31
113. A Correlative Modern Scientific Interpretation of the Concept of 'Prana' as described in the book- 'Yog Vidnyan, Part 1, Author-Unknown, Pages 317-322, Published by the Shri Pitambara Peeth, Datia, Madhya Pradesh, 4 th Edition, 2014. Whats App and e-Mail circulated Document January 2021.
Anil Vishnu Moharir.
114. What Does the Perfectly Scientific Sanatan Dharma Stand For?
Anil Vishnu Moharir
An article internationally circulated on WhatsApp and E-Mail December 2020.
Also Published in "In Quest of Bharateeya Shikshan' A Bi-Monthly Magazine of the Maharashtra Bharateeya Shikshan Mandal, Mumbai Vol. 30 No. 04, July-August 2021, pp 25-31.
115. Work, its Origin, Kinds and the Law of Karma: A Synthesis of their Scientific Foundation and Obligations for Human Survival
Anil Vishnu Moharir
Reprinted from 'In Quest of Bharateeya Shikshan' Vol. 30, Issue No. 06, November-December 2021, p30-39 continued from p 16-23, Jan-Feb 2022 Vol 31, issue-1 and concluded in the March-April 2022 issue from p 31-39.
116. A Scientific Basis of 'Samadhi'-A yogic feat of conditioning human body to a specific physiological state for experiencing a mentally 'blissful' condition: A note for critical appraisal.
A. V. Moharir, Submitted for publication April 2022.

- **BOOKS AUTHORED AND PUBLISHED**

1. 'ME MY OWN' English translation of the book " MEE MAJHA " Collection of 110 short poems by Chandrashekhar B. Gokhale.
Translated by Anil Vishnu Moharir, *"Aniruddha"*, from original in Marathi, Asuprakshi Publishers Pvt. 1997.
2. 'FOUR DECADES OF RESEARCH IN AGRICULTURAL PHYSICS-(1962-2002)'
A. V. Moharir Editor (Biophysics) and Chairman of the Editorial Committee, Division of Agricultural Physics, Indian Agricultural Research Institute, New Delhi, 2003.

3. 'PROFILE IN SOLITUDE' Felicitation of Dr. A. B. Joshi on is Ninety First Birthday', A. V. Moharir (Ed.), November 17, 2007, ISBN 978-81-7525-899-0. Pune
4. 'A LFE OF A PHYSICIST IN AGRICULTURAL RESEARCH' By A. V. Moharir, Published by the Author, 2013, pp 74, Price Rs. 300-00 + Postage Rs 60-00, ISBN 978-93-5126-183-4.
5. 'RANDOM WALKS IN SOLITUDE: Essays in Multidisciplinary Explorations in Science' By A. V. Moharir, Published by the Author, 2013, pp 173, Price Rs. 400-00 + Postage Rs 90-00, ISBN 978-93-5137-154-0.
6. 'A SCIENTIFIC LOOK AT THE CONCEPT OF SOUL: An Attempted Synthesis' By Anil Vishnu Moharir, Foreword By Prof Dr. Ravin Lakshman Thatte, M.S. FRCS (Edinburg), ZORBA BOOKS, Gurugram, 2017, pp 118, ISBN 978-93-5265-930-2.
7. 'VIJAY VISHNU MOHARIR: My Guardian Brother And A Sincere Philosopher Guide – A Free Expression of My Thoughts on the Eve of His Seventyfifth Birthday' By Anil Vishnu Moharir, October 07, 2017, Pune. Published by the Author for Private Circulation, pp 35.
8. 'A SCIENTIFIC LOOK AT THE CONCEPTS OF SOUL, REBIRTH, WORK AND THE LAW OF KARMA: An Attempted Synthesis' By Anil Vishnu Moharir with Foreword by Swami Supernanand, Secretary and Chairman, Ram Krishna Mission Institute of Culture, Kolkata. Zorba Books, Haryana, India 2019, pp 136. ISBN 978-93-88497-84-8.
9. 'HALF A CENTURY OF WALKING MY LIFE TOGETHER WITH SULOCHANA ANIL MOHARIR (nee-Sulochana Balkrishna Thakar): Golden Jubilee of Togetherness-1972-2022'. By Anil Vishnu Moharir. Published on the eve of the Golden Jubilee of the Marriage Anniversary on January 31, 2022, Pune, Maharashtra. Booklet for private circulation.

- **BOOK REVIEWES PUBLISHED By A.V. Moharir**

1. "Wings of Fire" An Autobiography by A. P. J. Abdul Kalam with Arun Tiwari, Universities Press, 3-5-819, Hyderguda, Hyderabad - 500 029, PP 189, Rs.200/-
   Business Inn Journal, 1999, Vol.20 No.1, PP 28-30. (ONE OF THE FIRST PUBLISHED REVIEWS ON THE BIOGRAPHY)
2. "Nuclear Radiation Detectors" by S. S. Kapur and V. S. Ramamurthy John Wiley & Sons (Wiley Eastern Ltd) New Delhi pp 236 Rs.35/-
3. Science Reporter, Vol. 24 No. 5 May 1987 p 315.
4. "Molecular Spectroscopy" by P. S. Sidhu
5. Tata McGraw-Hill Co.Ltd. New Delhi, 1985pp352, Science Reporter, Vol.23 No. 5 May 1986 p 351.
6. "Nuclear Radiation : Risks and Benefits " by Edward Pochlin

7. Clarendon Press, Oxford, 1985 paperback, pp 197, Science Reporter, Vol. 26 No. 2 February 1989 pp 114-115.
8. "Aspects of Radiation Biophysics " by Anjali Mookerjee and Sukhendu B.Bhattacharya,Environmental Science Series, Edited by B. Bhatia and
9. C. K. Varshney, **Science** Reporter, Vol. 25 No. 3 March 1988 p 182.
10. "Elements of Nuclear Physics : by W. E. Burcham, ELBS/ Longman,
11. 1988 Soft cover paperback pp 409, Pounds 4.00, Science Reporter, Vol. 26 No. 5, 1989 p 300.
12. "Isotopes in the Atomic Age " by Hari Jeevan Arnikar, Wiley Eastern Ltd. 4835/24 Ansari Road, Darya Ganj, New Delhi, pp 266 Rs 150/-,
13. Hardcover, Science Reporter, Vol. 27 No. 3, 1990 p 61.
14. "AAKAR - Janmaa Katha Shilpanchee " In Marathi Language, (Forms- The Story of the Birth of Sculptures) By Internationally Renowned Sculptor of India, Shri Sadashiv Sathe, Rajhansa Prakashan, Sadashiv Peth, Pune, Maharashtra 2001.
15. "Cotton Fibre Selection and Grading" Arindam Basu and K. P. Chellamani, 2004, Sounth India Textile Research Association, Coimbatore, India, pp 136, Hard Cover, ISBN No. 81-89139-12-6, Price Rs. 250/-(non members) Rs. 180/- (members), Indian J. Fibre & Textile Res. (CSIR) 2005, Vol. 30, pp 230-232.
16. "Himalayan Snow and Glaciers : Associated Environmental Problems, Progress and Prospects" Jagdish Bahadur, Concept Publishing Company, New Delhi, 2004, 164 pp, Price Rs. 300/- , Current Science, Vol 90, No. 6, 25 March 2006, pp 862-863.

- **CHAPTER WRITTEN FOR BOOK (International Edition)**

'Development and Structure-Property Relationships in Native Cotton' By Anil Vishnu Moharir, In "Progress in Textiles: Science and Technology, Vol 2 : Textile Fibres : Developments and Innovations, Series Editor Prof. V. K. Kothari, (1999) IAFL Publications, Volumes 1-7, New Delhi, India, pp 680- 735.

OTHER CONTRIBUTION MADE BY A. V. Moharir

Translated into English the following lectures and poems of Swami Ram of Jullundhar-Punjab from original in Hindi for the Swami Ram Trust-New Delhi for the Swami Ram Centenary Volumes Published in 2002 - 2003.

(I) 'Letter to Narayanrao from Ludhiana'

(II) 'This World is a Battle Field (Lecture No 14)'

(III) 'Materialism and the Supreme Self (Lecture No. 19)'

(IV) 'Flute of the Union (Poem)'

(V) 'Song of Life (Poem)'

THE EMBLEMS DESIGNED By Dr. A. V. Moharir and adopted by the institutions

1. Designed the Emblem for the Nuclear Research Laboratory, IARI and this has been officially adopted. The emblem beautifully depicts the basic mandate and profile of the work being done by the laboratory using nuclear tools.

2. Designed the Emblem for the Division of Agricultural Physics, IARI that philosophically signify the entire domain of research and teaching activities within the discipline of a hybrid discipline such as "Agricultural Physics ".
3. Designed the Emblem for the Society of Scientific Values, New Delhi-India under the Presidentship of Prof. A. S. Paintal, FNI, FRS, Director General, Indian Council of Medical Research (ICMR).

- **DESIGNED AND WRITTEN SCRIPT FOR THE FIRST EVER INFORMATION FOLDER PRINTED BY THE DIVISION OF AGRICULTURAL PHYSICS-IARI, NEW DELHI in 2001**

1. Wrote the Script for the Divisional Information Folder brought out for the first time at the time of the 88 th Indian Science Congress 2001 held at IARI, describing brief history of the division, its sphere of activities, type of research problems, specialization's available etc. and got the folders printed for wide distribution and circulation. (Copy of the pamphlet enclosed)
2. Ground Paper for Directors Comments Prepared for the Mini Symposium held to Mark the National Science Day on 28 th February 2001, "Removing Barriers for Interdisciplinary Research in Agriculture: A Time for Action", organized in association with the Delhi Chapter- Indian National Science Academy.

Summary Statement on the Contribution of Dr. Anil Vishnu Moharir to Science

Anil Vishnu Moharir (b: February 04, 1944 at Nagpur), holds B.Sc. (Physics, Chemistry, Mathematics) and M.Sc. (Physics) degrees from the Jiwaji University Gwalior and Ph.D. degree from the Indian Institute of Technology-Delhi. He started his scientific research career from the National Physical Laboratory in 1967 and was engaged in the project for preparing Selenium photoconductive cells under the guidance of Dr. V. G. Bhide, then Deputy Director, NPL. He joined the Indian Council of Agricultural Research (ICAR) Service in December 1968 and served in various capacities as Senior Research Assistant, Scientist, Principal Scientist, Professor and Head, Division of Agricultural Physics. He worked on spectroscopic, spectro-photometric and electron microscopic studies of soils, plants and other biological materials and developed accurate spectro-photometric methods for trace determination of Iron and Titanium, which have now been listed in text books of analytical chemistry. As a practicing electron microscopist, he developed many innovative, sample processing techniques for practical transmission electron microscopy of biological materials and developed a new procedure 'Contact Electron Micrography' for characterization of paper and thin film materials. Based on his studies on 'Moisture Hysteresis Curves of Seeds of Cereal Crops', he developed a simple laboratory procedure for screening drought tolerant wheat and rice varieties for cultivation under rain-fed conditions and introduced a new concept of 'Normalized-Moisture-Hysteresis' for comparative evaluation of genotypes, which has found practical use in bakery and biscuit industry in increasing the shelf life of bakery products by DANONE Biscuits, Belgium.

Later, he studied the fine structure and structure-property relationships in native cotton fibres of all the four commercially cultivated species *(Gossypium- herbaceum, Gossypium arboretum, Gossypium hirsutm and Gossypium barbadense)* for helping cotton breeders in selecting parent genotypes for evolving new strains with inherent high fibre tenacity through genetic hybridization as demanded by the modern high speed cotton processing and Open-End Spinning (OES Or Rotor Spinning) technology. From X-Ray diffraction studies on cotton fibres, he identified Hermans Cellulose Crystallite Orientation Index to be the best parameter for characterization of cotton for tensile strength of fibres, within individual *diploid* and *tetraploid* species and within a mixture of all species taken together. He has published over one hundred thirty research papers in national and international journals, presented several at conferences held in India, Germany, Belgium and USA as an invited 'Keynote Speaker'. He has translated and edited several books, poems, religious texts from Hindi and Marathi into English and served as Honorary Editor of the Indian Journal of Fibre and Textile Research (CSIR), New Delhi, Journal of Agricultural Research Karnal, Haryana, India, Chief Editor of the Journal of Agricultural Physics, New Delhi, and a regular referee for other scientific journals and as a Panel Scientist for the e-Text Book project of the National Institute of Science Communication (NISCOM-CSIR) New Delhi.

A recipient of prestigious fellowships from the IAEA, Vienna and the Commission of the European Communities, Brussels, Prof. Moharir has handled two international collaborative research projects on structure-property relationship in native cotton. He has travelled in England, Europe, Russia (USSR) and USA. Over half a dozen biographical compilations have listed him, consecutively for over a decade for his contribution to science. Interested in Hindustani classical music, Prof. Moharir is himself an accomplished portrait artist in charcoal medium. In New Delhi, he had been actively associated with various social, educational and cultural organizations and served the prominent the Maratha Mitra Mandal in various capacities as member of the Executive Committee, Joint Secretary and Secretary for over twenty long years under presidentship of Late Shri Annasaheb (A. P.) Shinde and Shri Shankarrao B. Chavan.

After retirement in 2006, he is regularly writing freelance on scientific subjects from multi-disciplinary angles. His book- 'Profile in Solitude- Felicitation of Professor Atmaram Bhairav (A. B.) Joshi on his Ninety first Birthday' with Foreword from Professor M. S. Swaminathan, FRS, FNA, is a *de-facto* national document on the life and contribution of Dr. Atmaram Bhairav (A. B.) Joshi, to the first Green Revolution. His other books- 'A Life of a Physicist in Agricultural Research' and 'Random Walks in Solitude-Essays in Multidisciplinary Explorations in Science' are unique and scholarly contributions to science. His books –'A Scientific Look at the Concept of Soul: An Attempted Synthesis', Zorba Books, Gurugram, India 2017 and 'A Scientific Look at the Concepts of Soul, Rebirth, Work and the Law of Karma: An Attempted Synthesis' Zorba Books, Second Revised and enlarged edition 2019 are the scholarly, innovative, multidisciplinary interpretations, based on modern science, of the ancient concepts of Soul, Rebirth, Work and the Law of Karma.

Professor Moharir served as a member of the National Panel of Eminent Citizens, Ministry of Rural Development, Government of India, for evaluation of the projects executed under the Mahatma Gandhi National Rural Employment Guarantee Scheme (MGNREGA) in the state of Nagaland for over two years.

After living and serving for 76 years in New Delhi, Dr Moharir has finally come for permanent settlement in Pune since February 2021.

www.ingramcontent.com/pod-product-compliance
Ingram Content Group UK Ltd.
Pitfield, Milton Keynes, MK11 3LW, UK
UKHW041825200726
13854UKWH00002BA/558

9 789393 029201